WHAT

HAPPENS WHEN

YOU DIE?

What the Bible Reveals
about the Next Life

FR. JOHN WAISS

BEACON PUBLISHING
North Palm Beach, Florida

Design by Madeline Harris
Interior by Ashley Wirfel

ISBN: 978-1-929266-59-3 (softcover)
ISBN: 978-1-929266-60-9 (e-book)

Library of Congress Cataloging-in-Publication Data
Names: Waiss, John R., 1957- author.
Title: What happens when you die? : what the Bible reveals
about the next life / Fr. John Waiss.
Description: North Palm Beach, Florida : Beacon Publishing, Inc., 2017.
Identifiers: LCCN 2017028962 | ISBN 9781929266593 (softcover) | ISBN
9781929266609 (e-book)
Subjects: LCSH: Future life—Christianity. | Future life—Biblical teaching.
Classification: LCC BT903 .W34 2017 | DDC
236/.2—dc23

For more information on this title or other books and CDs available through the
Dynamic Catholic Book Program,
please visit www.DynamicCatholic.com.

The Dynamic Catholic Institute
5081 Olympic Blvd • Erlanger • Kentucky • 41018
Phone: 1–859–980–7900
Email: info@DynamicCatholic.com

First printing, September 2017

Printed in the United States of America

CONTENTS

INTRODUCTION
1

ONE
Death—A Blessing or a Curse?
5

TWO
Heaven—An Awesome Place?
19

THREE
To Hell with Hell?
39

FOUR
Sin Is Hell
51

FIVE
Am I Really Ready for Heaven?
68

SIX
Purifying Fire
80

SEVEN
Can Non-Christians Be Saved?
90

EIGHT
It's Your Choice!
101

NOTES
105

INTRODUCTION

Why write about heaven and hell, especially when today many consider these topics irrelevant, or mythical at best? Science and technology enables modern man to dominate the world of nature. Advances in biology have reached the point of understanding and controlling the mechanisms of life, even explaining how the brain and thought processes work (although freedom still eludes us). This seems to eliminate any place for the soul and the afterlife, making talk about heaven and hell a waste of time or an impossible dream.

Science seems to have relegated heaven and hell to a fantasy world of wishful thinking belonging to the unsophisticated and uneducated masses. Sociologists consider heaven and hell a human invention used to describe what people could not know about life and death. Thus, "primitive" human beings tried to avoid facing the nothingness of death by inventing the "myth" of heaven and hell. But because science explains death "objectively" as the breakdown of a biological machine, death has become a meaningless moment. And if death has little or no meaning, then *life* has little or no meaning.

Besides, talk of heaven and hell seems to make many of us feel very uncomfortable, perhaps even angry. Yet, surprisingly, this topic interests many people. The weekly newsmagazine *U.S. News and World Report* does a special cover story on it every few years. Often the article consists of a survey of how many people believe in hell, how many in heaven, what it takes to get in, and so on. Then the authors interview a number of so-called experts to give their opinions about the results of the survey and what heaven and hell might be like if they were to exist. Why does the magazine feature this type of story so frequently? Because this topic interests people—it sells magazines!

But for believers it matters little what the so-called experts opine. What matters is what God has revealed. And perhaps this interests unbelievers as well, just in case God's revelation may make more sense than their own theories and hypotheses.

This book arose from an incident that happened to me several years ago. I was talking with an eighth-grade boy. He wasn't Catholic; his parents had had him baptized in a Christian denomination, but the whole family had long since stopped going to church. It just occurred to me to ask him, "Mike, if you knew whether heaven and hell existed, do you think it would make any difference in how you lived your life?"

Without hesitation, he replied, "You bet! It would make a big difference!" Implied in this was the awareness that if he truly knew, then he would live his life to make sure he avoided hell and made it to heaven.

I then asked him, "Don't you think you'd better find out?"

I encouraged him to begin reading the Bible to see what it says about heaven and hell. I especially encouraged him to look at what Jesus said about the subject. If anyone should know about heaven and hell it would be Christ, since "no one has ascended into heaven but he who descended from heaven, the Son of man" (John 3:13). If Jesus Christ truly came from and returned to heaven, then he is best suited to tell us about this eternal reality.

This book is intended to provide people like Mike with a simple guide to help sort out what Scripture says about the afterlife. I also intend to address some of the questions people pose to challenge Christian teaching on this subject. If we cannot address those questions, then we cannot fully witness to our belief in Jesus Christ or make the daily decisions needed to help others get to heaven and avoid hell.

I do not pretend to cover all the questions regarding heaven, hell, and the afterlife. That would mean a much more extensive book that nobody would want to read. I want to keep this short and to the point, addressing the most pressing questions in the minds of people today.

Since both Protestant and Catholic Christians need to be able to answer these questions, I have tried to write this book in a form that is useful and challenging to both—some Bible expressions will be challenging to Catholics and others to non-Catholics. In the end, wrestling with these ideas and what the Bible says about heaven and hell will help bring all Christians closer together and give us a better mutual understanding of the biblical roots we share.

I am especially grateful to the students at Antonian College Preparatory High School in San Antonio, Texas, who challenged me with many of the questions I address in this book. They made me think, search the Scriptures, and pray that the Holy Spirit would guide my efforts. I would also like to thank the many individuals who read the manuscript in various phases. Your insightful comments, questions, and corrections are much appreciated.

ONE

Death—A Blessing or a Curse?

Death is a great mystery. The mere possibility of it—our own or our loved ones'—often terrifies us. We hate death, because it takes us away from those we love. So, many prefer not to think or talk about it. It's easier just to ignore it. However, death is part of life, and we cannot avoid it.

The Bible tells us that death entered the world with sin—the sin of Adam and Eve:

> Therefore as sin came into the world through one man and death through sin, and so death spread to all men because all men sinned. . . . [B]ecause of one man's trespass, death reigned through that one man . . . to condemnation for all men. (Romans 5:12, 17–18)

We long to live—and live longer. We desire that our friends and family not part from us. So it's natural to ask: Why would God punish us with death? Couldn't he have allowed us to go on living forever? Couldn't he have found a less dreadful way to punish us?

Some get angry with God when a loved one dies, especially if the loved one was a young child. "Why did you allow this person to die? Why didn't you answer my prayers and save this person's life? Why, why, why?"

God has a joy-filled answer for us, if we are willing to listen.

THE TRAIN OF LIFE

There is a famous story about Oliver Wendell Holmes, a former Supreme Court judge.

One day Holmes got on a train leaving Washington, D.C., and took a seat. Not wanting to waste a moment, he opened his briefcase and began working. Perhaps it was some case he was reviewing for the court. At any rate, he got absorbed in his work and lost awareness of his surroundings.

Soon the train started its journey down the tracks and the conductor began checking people's tickets, going down the aisle seat by seat. When he came to Holmes, he interrupted the judge with, "May I see your ticket, sir?"

Stirred as if from a stupor, the judge mumbled, "Ticket? Oh, yes, my ticket!" He then began to check his pockets, searching for his train ticket. He checked his pants, his shirt, his jacket, and finally began emptying his briefcase and rummaging through his papers.

As the conductor recognized the famous passenger, he tried to calm him down. "Your Honor, please, don't worry about your ticket. You are an honorable person, so when you get to your destination and you find it, just send it to us in the mail."

But Judge Holmes was not deterred. He continued his search, now more anxious than ever. Again the conductor, wanting to help in some way, said, "Your Honor, we trust you. Don't worry about your ticket."

"But you don't understand!" the judge quipped. "I don't know where I'm going! I need that ticket!"

This funny and true story seems to be a great metaphor for people today. All of us are traveling together on the "train of life," heading down the tracks that will lead to our ultimate destiny. Many seem to be on the train with no clue where they are going, where the train will stop and let them off. Perhaps on this train, they, like Oliver Wendell Holmes, are absorbed in their work. Or perhaps they are in the dining car enjoying a good meal, or in the sleeper getting caught up on their rest, or in one of the seats looking out the window at the scenery as life passes them by. So many of our fellow passengers don't know where they are going.

But at some point this train is going to stop for each one of us and we will be asked to get off. Where will that be? Heaven? Hell? Nothingness?

GOD'S WAKE-UP CALL

One thing we can say is that death gives each one of us an opportunity to stop and think. Perhaps we have a brush with death—a serious illness, accident, or near-accident. Perhaps we experience the death of a loved one, a fellow worker or student, or someone we just happened to hear about. In such cases, death can be a kind of wake-up call, a reminder that each of us will eventually die, and we will have to face the reality of what happens after death.

Experiencing the possibility of death causes us to ask ourselves, "If I were to die today, what would happen? Where would

I go? Would it be heaven? Hell? Would I just cease to exist, simply drop off into some kind of oblivion or nothingness?"

Now is the time to ask those questions. God doesn't want us to become like the foolish maidens who were not ready to meet their master:

> "Then the kingdom of heaven shall be compared to ten maidens who took their lamps and went to meet the bridegroom. Five of them were foolish, and five were wise. For when the foolish took their lamps, they took no oil with them; but the wise took flasks of oil with their lamps. As the bridegroom was delayed, they all slumbered and slept. But at midnight there was a cry, 'Behold, the bridegroom! Come out to meet him.' Then all those maidens rose and trimmed their lamps. And the foolish said to the wise, 'Give us some of your oil, for our lamps are going out.' But the wise replied, 'Perhaps there will not be enough for us and for you; go rather to the dealers and buy for yourselves.' And while they went to buy, the bridegroom came, and those who were ready went in with him to the marriage feast; and the door was shut. Afterward the other maidens came also, saying, 'Lord, lord, open to us.' But he replied, 'Truly, I say to you, I do not know you.' Watch therefore, for you know neither the day nor the hour." (Matthew 25:1–13)

The foolish maidens failed to look ahead. They did not anticipate what was needed for the hereafter, and therefore they missed it. But God does not want us to experience this same letdown. He allows us to face the possibility of death now, in order to wake us up from our slumber. He gives us the opportunity to wake up so we can get enough "oil" for our encounter with him and actually look forward to it!

PASSING GLORY

It's so easy for us to become absorbed in our day-to-day activities as we try to survive and make a life for ourselves. Often we set high goals and admire great accomplishments, whether they are our own or someone else's. God uses death and disaster to remind us that these things are all temporary.

> And as [Jesus] came out of the temple, one of his disciples said to him, "Look, Teacher, what wonderful stones and what wonderful buildings!" And Jesus said to him, "Do you see these great buildings? There will not be left here one stone upon another, that will not be thrown down." (Mark 13:1–2)

I imagine a modern-day Christian pointing out to Jesus not the Temple but the great modern creations of man: skyscrapers, the Golden Gate Bridge, jumbo jets, big-screen TVs, modern computers, smartphones, satellite communication, the space shuttle, the Internet. Jesus would probably respond in a similar way—"Who do you think you are? There will not be left here one stone upon another, that will not be thrown down"—making us aware of the transient nature of these accomplishments.

Death puts all our work and plans into perspective. We can spend so much time and effort fooling ourselves that we are building up our little empire, our castle, our temple . . . but death puts all those efforts back into perspective, as Jesus said so succinctly:

> And he told them a parable, saying, "The land of a rich man brought forth plentifully; and he thought to himself, 'What shall I do, for I have nowhere to store my crops?' And he said, 'I will do this: I will

pull down my barns, and build larger ones; and there I will store all my grain and my goods. And I will say to my soul, Soul, you have ample goods laid up for many years; take your ease, eat, drink, be merry.' But God said to him, 'Fool! This night your soul is required of you; and the things you have prepared, whose will they be?' So is he who lays up treasure for himself, and is not rich toward God." (Luke 12:16–21)

In 1989, the Loma Prieta earthquake hit the San Francisco Bay Area. A striking video clip was taken from a car that was traveling east on the Bay Bridge. Traffic was at a standstill because a section of the upper deck had collapsed onto the lower deck. To get people off the bridge, the police started routing cars that were traveling east on the lower deck onto the upper deck at Yerba Buena Island so that they could head west to San Francisco and find an alternate route to the East Bay.

However, the drivers of some of the first cars got disoriented and started going east on the upper deck. The people in one car had sensed that something was wrong, stopped, and began recording what happened next. They were filming the condition of the collapsed section of the bridge just as another car sped past them, careening off the collapsed portion of the bridge to death and destruction. It happened so fast that nobody could do anything to stop the errant driver, who obviously thought she was in control.

This incident can be symbolic of how many people take the wrong direction in their lives, so often unaware of the consequences. And beyond that of physical death, another consequence awaits: God calls each of us to give an account of our life.

Another consequence of the Loma Prieta earthquake was how packed the churches were right after the disaster struck—even in San Francisco! People knew they needed God. Yet in just two months the attendance surge was no longer perceivable; for most, life resumed its normal, carefree existence as their need for God faded.

Jesus reminds us how death and disaster should get us to think, lest we forget that this life is not the end:

> There were some present at that very time who told him of the Galileans whose blood Pilate had mingled with their sacrifices. And [Jesus] answered them, "Do you think that these Galileans were worse sinners than all the other Galileans, because they suffered thus? I tell you, No; but unless you repent you will all likewise perish. Or those eighteen upon whom the tower in Silo'am fell and killed them, do you think that they were worse offenders than all the others who dwelt in Jerusalem? I tell you, No; but unless you repent you will all likewise perish." (Luke 13:1–5)

According to Jesus, death and disaster hit these individuals not because they were sinners, but to remind the rest of us that we too will die. Death is God's wake-up call. Instead of being a horrible punishment as a result of sin, it's really God's gift to get us to stop what we are doing and think about where our lives are really going.

A WORLD WITHOUT DEATH

Can you imagine what the world would be like without death— if people such as Hitler and Stalin remained on earth exercising their tyranny without the fear of ever dying? Is that the kind of world you would care to inherit, where selfishness and pride go unchecked until there's no chance of reform?

We shouldn't fear death; instead we should see it as an opportunity to assess our own lives, as a way to discern where we are really going. Truly this is God's mercy in action. He foresaw how easily we can get caught up in this earthly life and forget about the eternal life he wants for us as his children. Death is God's means of directing us beyond the present moment and immediate pleasure, so that we may consider our actions in light of eternity.

We don't have to fear death because through his death and resurrection, Christ destroyed "him who has the power of death, that is, the devil" (Hebrews 2:14). Death is a great reminder that "here we have no lasting city, but we seek the city which is to come" (Hebrews 13:14).

In my own life, I can attest to the impact of people I knew who met with death suddenly and unexpectedly. I remember quite vividly a college student named Tom, who had just turned nineteen (I was twenty-two at the time). One evening he visited the Opus Dei center where I lived and worked, in order to visit with the priest and go to confession. A number of us were decorating the center for Christmas when he came over to give us a hand. After he left, he went home and was having a snack with his parents. He blacked out and fell over backward in the chair. His parents rushed him to the hospital, but there was little that could be done, and he died. He'd had a massive brain hemorrhage. Here was a young man God called home just after he had given an account of his life to him in confession. What a wonderful way to go!

And yet I was shaken by the suddenness of his passing. God used this event to speak to me, to help me to take stock of where my life was going. Was I prepared to leave everything and meet my Maker? Was I really looking forward to it?

LIVING OUR LAST DAY

Live each day as though it were your last . . . and your last day as though you would live forever. This is really how a Christian lives, with the awareness that we may go to meet God at any moment:

> "Watch therefore, for you do not know on what day your Lord is coming. But know this, that if the householder had known in what part of the night the thief was coming, he would have watched and would not have let his house be broken into. Therefore you also must be ready; for the Son of man is coming at an hour you do not expect." (Matthew 24:42–44; see 1 Thessalonians 5:1–3)

You may think: *If I knew that I were going to die tomorrow, I would spend all day in church, praying and getting myself ready.* But would you? Wouldn't you spend time with your family, letting them know how much you loved them, asking for forgiveness for the times you hurt them, and forgiving them for any hurt they caused you? Wouldn't you try to have a good conversation with that coworker who is a bit lost? Wouldn't you also try to be cheerful, not make a big deal about silly little annoyances, and leave an image of a happy and generous soul in the mind of those with whom you engaged? Certainly you would want Jesus to know that he is numero uno in your life by spending sufficient time in prayer, making a good confession, attending Mass, and receiving Communion. But you would also want to show him that you were doing your best to fulfill the mission he had entrusted to you.

Death allows us to discover the true meaning of everything we do and everything that happens to us in life. It puts earthly pleasure in its very relative place. Let's thank God for his wonderful mercy in granting us this wake-up call that can frame and put into perspective the little nothings that make up our day. As the apostle Paul said, "For to me to live is Christ, and to die is gain" (Philippians 1:21).

QUESTIONS AND ANSWERS

Why do we fear death?

There are many reasons we fear death. First, because of our limited vision, we love earthly life and don't want to let go of what we already have. We also fear the unknown and worry about what it will be like after we die. Perhaps we see how often we fall short in our lives and find it hard to imagine a Father who would ever forgive us for all our sins and failings. Thus, we fear the possibility of hell. Perhaps we also have seen the horrible death of a loved one, or just some ugly scenes in a movie or on TV, making death seem like a frightening reality instead of a pathway to the arms of Jesus.

But the more we grow in our faith and in our relationship with God, the less we fear death, because he reassures us of the joy awaiting us if we faithfully respond to his grace and trust in his love.

Why does it feel like God is punishing us when someone close to us dies?

Well, death *is* a kind of punishment. It's God's response to the sin of our first parents, Adam and Eve, who chose to live their life independent of him. They chose not to respect God's plan for creation by deciding for themselves what they thought was good and bad, independent of his loving commands.

Yet God did not send us death simply to make us suffer, but to help us understand the consequences of our actions: If we live our life independent of him, we kill our relationship with him. Sin is separation from God, and it produces spiritual death.

Death also contains a call. The more loved ones we have in heaven, the more we want to join them. We think less of pursuing our own selfish interests, we become less attached to the things of this world, and we begin thinking about what we need to do to be with our beloved grandparents, parents, brothers, sisters, and friends.

In a sense, death is a punishment that truly heals us.

Why did God punish us for the sin of Adam and Eve? Why should we have to pay for their sin?

The original sin of Adam and Eve caused a break in their relationship with God, which affected his relationship with all their descendants.

One way to look at it is to imagine your earthly father having a very close relationship with the president of the United States.

Consequently, you and your siblings can visit the White House anytime you want, roam the building, and explore the grounds, simply because your father is a friend and confidant of the president.

One day, however, your father betrays the president; he is no longer allowed to return to the White House. Would you and your siblings still have free access to the White House? No, of course not. That was a privilege you had because of your father's relationship, not because you had some right to it. You are not being punished for any sin your father committed; you simply lost a privilege to which you never had a right.

Original sin is similar. When Adam and Eve sinned, we lost the privilege of not dying; we lost the privilege of an intimate friendship with God. Fortunately, Christ came to restore what was lost by demonstrating the true meaning of life through his death on the cross.

What happens when you die, especially if you don't know what to believe in? Where do you go?

No one really knows what death is like. There have been many people who have had near-death experiences, but exactly what happens when we die is a mystery. Only God knows.

Hopefully, as you read this book, you will get a clearer idea of what may or may not happen to you—whether you want to believe it or not. God leaves each one of us free to respond to his revelation.

How do you explain death to a little child?

One mother explained it this way: "You know how sometimes

you fall asleep in my arms or in my lap, only to wake up in your bed? You don't know how you got there, but somehow you did.

"When we die, the opposite happens. You fall asleep in your bed or wherever you are, and you wake up in the arms of God, experiencing the great joy of being with the one who loves us more than any other."

Is it wrong to want to die?

The desire to die and be with God is not bad in itself, as long as we do not use it to escape from our responsibilities, from fulfilling God's mission for us. Sometimes our lives may seem to be failures, or we are suffering so intensely that death seems like the only option. Elijah felt that way after purifying Israel of the prophets of Baal and being persecuted by the political powers for his role:

> Ahab told Jezebel all that Elijah had done, and how he had slain all the prophets with the sword. Then Jezebel sent a messenger to Elijah, saying, "So may the gods do to me and more also, if I do not make your life as the life of one of them by this time tomorrow." Then he was afraid, and he arose and . . . went a day's journey into the wilderness, and came and sat down under a broom tree; and he asked that he might die, saying, "It is enough; now, O LORD, take away my life; for I am no better than my fathers." (1 Kings 19:1–4)

St. Paul had similar sentiments:

> For we were so utterly, unbearably crushed that we despaired of life itself. Why, we felt that we had received the sentence of death; but

that was to make us rely not on ourselves but on God who raises the dead; . . . on him we have set our hope that he will deliver us again. (2 Corinthians 1:8–10)

It's not wrong to want to die, but we should abandon ourselves into the hands of God and allow him to show us what he wants of us while on this earth. We should never be afraid to live, because ultimately we live only by God's will and mercy.

TWO

Heaven—An Awesome Place?

Most people hope the train of life will eventually stop for them at heaven, although they may not be too eager to find out. Some don't seem to care. Others think everyone will go to heaven (except, perhaps, a few such as Hitler and Stalin), as long as they don't do anything *really* bad; they just can't imagine God being too severe.

Yet questions remain: What does it take to go to heaven? Will I go to heaven if I accept Jesus Christ as my Lord and Savior? How can I be sure? And what will heaven be like? Will I be married there? Will it be just me and Jesus, or will I interact with my family, friends, and important people in history? What will heaven mean to me? Will it truly encompass all beauty and happiness? Will it dispel all toil, pain, sorrow, tiredness, hunger, depression, and physical suffering (as Revelation 21:4 says)? Will it be free of dissension, anger, malice, loneliness, sadness, and despair?

DO YOU WANT TO GO TO HEAVEN?

Years ago I worked with junior high school boys. Often they, perhaps a bit intimidated by talking to a priest, seemed to have little to say. So I would ask questions to help break the ice and get them to open up a bit.

I specifically remember asking one student, "Do you want to go to heaven?"

He said, "No, not really," with a hint of wanting to end the conversation.

Surprised by his answer, I followed up with, "Why not? I thought everyone wanted to go to heaven."

With a face that showed his disinterest, he replied, "Well, the idea of sitting on a cloud and playing a harp for all eternity seems awfully boring to me."

Well, he was right on that score. I would react the same way if I had that idea about heaven. I thought quickly about how I could describe heaven in such a way that might pique the interest of a ten- or eleven-year-old. So I asked, "Do you want to know what heaven is really like?"

"What?"

"It's like going to Disneyland, only a hundred times better!"

His eyes got really wide as his head began to race with ideas about what that could mean, and he said, "Then I do want to go to heaven!"

I won that one! However, it occurred to me later that it was not the best description of heaven. Not that there won't be pleasure; certainly there will be. There may even be amusement park rides in heaven, or, as many adults like to describe it, "the great golf course in the sky."

Yet all these descriptions miss out on the *essence* of heaven. What makes heaven heavenly is not the fun or the physical pleasure that we hope to experience, but something much greater.

WHAT DID JESUS SAY ABOUT HEAVEN?

What is heaven really like? How did Jesus describe it? These are two of my favorite questions. When I ask them in a classroom setting, I often get perplexed looks, with students scratching their heads trying to find the answer. Jesus said a lot about hell, describing it as a furnace of unquenchable fire, outer darkness, or Gehenna, where people "weep and gnash their teeth" (see Matthew 13:42; 25:30, 41; Mark 9:43), but he said very little to describe heaven. But the little he said is worth paying attention to:

> "The kingdom of heaven may be compared to a king who gave a marriage feast for his son, and sent his servants to call those who were invited to the marriage feast . . . And those servants went out into the streets and gathered all whom they found, both bad and good; so the wedding hall was filled with guests." (Matthew 22:2–3, 10)

So, heaven is like a wedding feast!

Once, when I was describing this to a group, one person commented, "I can relate to that. I was at a wedding last week. They had an incredible reception: a lot of good food, good drink, a great band—everyone was dancing and having a wonderful time!"

And yet here we go again, focusing on physical pleasure. If we focus only on that, we will miss what is really important. We can start by asking, "Who is getting married?"

The answer seems obvious: the son of the great king—the Son of God, Christ. Yes, but to whom is he getting married? To the Church, Christ's spouse (see Ephesians 5:22–33). This means you and me, as members of the Church, Christ's Body.

Moreover, who is the happiest person at a wedding? Is it the father of the bride? Is it the bride's little sister, who will now have her own room? No, it's the bride. It's her big day! It's a defining moment in her life. Usually a bride changes her name; she moves from identifying herself by her relationship to her father, mother, and siblings to fully identifying herself by the new family she is forming and by her relationship to her husband, to whom she is called to "cleave." The happiness of heaven is the happiness of a bride at her wedding celebration, and that happiness will last forever. Heaven is the fullness of being that comes from a life of love.

Certainly in heaven there will be physical pleasure—eating, drinking, dancing, and the joy of others celebrating our good fortune—yet the principal reason for our happiness is experiencing fully a love that will never fail us, one that entails a complete personal union with God that will totally define our lives forever.

DOES EVERYONE GO TO HEAVEN?

When you understand that heaven entails entering the Church's spousal union with Christ, then it makes sense that not everyone will go to heaven. As Jesus clearly says:

"Not every one who says to me, 'Lord, Lord,' shall enter the kingdom of heaven, but he who does the will of my Father who is in heaven. On that day many will say to me, 'Lord, Lord, did we not prophesy in your name, and cast out demons in your name, and do many mighty works in your name?' And then will I declare to them, 'I never knew you; depart from me, you evildoers.'" (Matthew 7:21–23)

Certainly those who outright reject Jesus won't go to heaven. But these verses add something else: Not everyone who says they accept him will be there either. Some who taught with authority (prophesied) in Jesus' name will not make it to heaven. Some who helped others overcome their demons and slavery to sin will not make it. Some who did mighty works of mercy and charity will not make it either. Why? Because they did not do God's will.

What is God's will? Christ describes it in the preceding verses of the Sermon on the Mount, which begins with the Beatitudes, challenging us to be poor in spirit, meek, merciful, pure in heart, peacemakers, to hunger and thirst for righteousness, and to allow ourselves to be persecuted for righteousness' sake (Matthew 5:3–12); he challenges us to fulfill and teach all the commandments (5:19), and then raises the bar on each of the Ten Commandments (5:20–47), calling us to be perfect as God the Father is perfect (5:48). Jesus also encourages true prayer, almsgiving, and fasting as ways of laying up treasures in heaven (6:1–21), avoiding selfish materialism (6:22–34), and judging others (7:1–6). At the end of this, he says, "Not every one who says to me, 'Lord, Lord,' shall enter the kingdom of heaven, but he who does the will of my Father . . ." (7:21).

This all makes sense when one realizes that going to heaven means entering the Church's nuptial relationship with Christ, and recognizes that such a relationship requires love. As Pope Benedict XVI put it:

> Jesus himself is what we call "heaven"; heaven is not a place but a person, the person of him in whom God and man are forever and inseparably one. And we go to heaven and enter into heaven to the extent that we go to Jesus Christ and enter into him.[1]

Now, imagine you die and go before Jesus. You tell him, "Hey, Lord, I would like to go to heaven. It seems like an awesome place. It really sounds like a lot of fun, full of all kinds of pleasures! Can you let me in? Please?"

Jesus replies, "Oh, so you want to marry me? That's what heaven is really all about: the wedding feast of the Lamb—and I'm the Lamb—who marries the Church, my bride. Do you want to be one with me forever? Do you wish to enter into such a deep relationship with me?"

And since you desire heaven, you reply, "Sure, Lord, if that's what it takes. I'll join the Church for the ride. Now can you let me in? I can't wait to go."

Yet Jesus doesn't stop there. He asks you another question: "But do you truly love me? You see, this is not about a group hug, but a personal, total, permanent, and intimate relationship. I can't enter such a relationship with someone who doesn't love me. You must love me 'with all your heart, and with all your soul, and with all your mind, and with all your strength' (Mark 12:30)."

Since you're reading this book, you'll know how to answer that. So you say, "Okay, Lord, I love you—now will you let me in?"

"Prove it to me," Jesus replies. He continues, "Oh, by the way, we have recorded your life. Let's sit down together and watch that video, and you can point out the things you did out of love for me. . . . Don't worry, we have plenty of time."

So you sit down with Jesus and watch as your life passes before your eyes. You see all your selfish acts, your proud reactions, all the times when you were critical, unkind, or dishonest. You keep watching that video, waiting to point out something good to Jesus. Perhaps you ask to fast-forward through those portions of the video that show things you're ashamed of. But you view your whole life, a process familiar to many (including some saints) who have had a near-death experience. Hopefully you are able to show Jesus that you did not live only for yourself but also for him.

WE SHALL BE JUDGED ON OUR LOVE

In heaven we will see God face-to-face, with a love that's deeper and greater in intensity than anything we've ever experienced before. Divine love is what endures:

Love bears all things, believes all things, hopes all things, endures all things. Love never ends; as for prophecies, they will pass away; as for tongues, they will cease; as for knowledge, it will pass away. . . . [B]ut when the perfect comes, the imperfect will pass away. . . . For now we see in a mirror dimly, but then *face to face*. Now I know in part; then I shall understand fully, even as I have been fully understood. So faith, hope, love abide, these three; but the greatest of these is love. (1 Corinthians 13:7–13; emphasis added)

Jesus showed us this kind of love by suffering and dying on the cross: "Greater love has no man than this, that a man lay down his life for his friends" (John 15:13). He calls each one of us to love him in return as we enter the Church's intimate spousal relationship with him. We then are able to love one another in Christ.

"A new commandment I give to you, that you love one another; even as I have loved you, that you also love one another." (John 13:34)

[W]alk in love, as Christ loved us and gave himself up for us, a fragrant offering and sacrifice to God. (Ephesians 5:1–2)

By this we know love, that he laid down his life for us; and we ought to lay down our lives for the brethren. (1 John 3:16)

St. John of the Cross concludes, "At the evening of life, we shall be judged on our love."[2] Christ's gift to us and our gift to him is an eternal exchange of life-giving love!

This makes earthly life a kind of courtship with our Lord, or better yet, a time of betrothal to him in preparation for the wedding feast and our ultimate union with him. If some little girls begin to plan and prepare for their weddings while in grade school, it's not too early for us to begin our preparation for heaven, where we will see the love of our eternal life face-to-face. And while we are still on earth, we will develop a deep desire to please him as best as we can.

So heaven involves a lot more than we ever realized. Entering into the Church's eternal marital relationship with Jesus will be infinite bliss—beyond anything we can imagine. Then let's love him as he deserves now, while we're here on earth. Let's respond with love to that never-ending love by seeking him first above all else while carrying out our earthly affairs. Then when Christ calls us to the wedding feast, we "who are in the tombs will hear his voice and come forth, those who have done good, to the resurrection of life" (John 5:28–29), because we have shown our love for our beloved by doing our best to fulfill his purpose for us day after day.

DEATH REVISITED

We saw how death is a profound mystery that draws us to take stock of our life, see the limit of our active mission on earth, and consider where we may end up. As long as we are alive, we still have a mission to fulfill. But for a Christian it means more than that. The *Catechism of the Catholic Church* says it's actually a participation in Christ's death—and a share in his resurrection (see *CCC,* 1006)!

Christ's death marked the fulfillment of his earthly life and revealed the greatness of his love for us: "Greater love has no man than this, that a man lay down his life for his friends" (John 15:13). As St. John Paul II explains:

> The Paschal Mystery . . . completely reveals the spousal love of God. Christ is the Bridegroom because "he has given himself": his body has been "given," his blood has been "poured out" (see Luke

22:19–20). In this way "he loved them to the end" (John 13:1). The "sincere gift" contained in the Sacrifice of the Cross gives definitive prominence to the spousal meaning of God's love.[3]

Christ's love on the cross is spousal because it's total; there he gives us his whole life and self. His death, then, is the ultimate sign of the love that will be consummated in heaven. Our death too can show our love for Christ. It can be our ultimate gift to him, following in his footsteps.

In any gift, one transfers dominion over the object given to the recipient. This is the nature of a gift. If I give my friend a hundred-dollar bill, then I relinquish dominion over it as my friend takes it. Something changes in the hundred-dollar bill when it is given—but what changes is not physical; what changes is who has dominion over the bill. If someone steals the bill, then I still have legal dominion over it and can demand it by furnishing proof of ownership in a court of law. But if I give it away as a gift, then I have no legal or moral claim over the hundred-dollar bill.

What makes death such a powerful act is that what is being offered to the recipient as a gift is the very life of the giver: Christ gives his whole human and divine life for each one of us. But it calls each one of us to respond by the gift of our own life to him. Thus each one of us can view our own death as an opportunity to make ourselves a gift, to give our whole self to Christ. Death is the opportunity everyone has to relinquish dominion over his own life so as to form something new—a new creation (see 2 Corinthians 5:17). By letting go of the control of our life, we form the new life of communion as one body and one spirit in Christ (see 1 Corinthians 12:13).

So we see that for us it's not about avoiding death at all costs—instead it's about living our lives in ways that show God how much we love him. It's about being ready to give ourselves completely to him when he calls us to him.

QUESTIONS AND ANSWERS

Where would we go after we died if God didn't exist?

If God didn't exist, then we wouldn't exist. If we did not exist, then we wouldn't have to worry about dying. Also, if God didn't exist, then entering into a spiritual union with him would be impossible. So there would be no heaven and there would be no hell. But if there were no God, heaven, or hell, then we would not have any responsibility for our actions. There would be neither good nor evil—murder, child abuse, and rape would all have the same neutral moral value as helping the poor and heroic self-sacrifice for one's family.

What proof do we have of heaven?

What proof do you have that someone truly loves you and will be faithful to you in marriage? You have none. It's impossible to prove. You have to trust that person and see how his or her deeds back up his or her words.

The way we know that God loves us and wants us to enter into an eternal relationship with him in heaven is by listening to his Word and seeing how he has been faithful to that Word throughout salvation history. So, believing in heaven is a matter of faith.

Do we have any idea of what heaven is like? Is it a place, or is it just a state of mind?

Heaven is more than a place. It's a very special relationship of the soul to Jesus Christ. Since Jesus rose with his body and entered heaven with a glorified body, his physical body must be in a physical place as well. And he tells us, "Where I am, there shall my servant be . . ." (John 12:26).

Although the essence of heaven entails this relationship to Christ, he also tells us:

> Let not your hearts be troubled; believe in God, believe also in me. In my Father's house are many rooms; if it were not so, would I have told you that I go to prepare a place for you? And when I go and prepare a place for you, I will come again and will take you to myself, that where I am you may be also. (John 14:1–3)

If you were a pure spirit with only a state of mind and no body, then Christ wouldn't need to prepare a room for you. Heaven is to be where Christ is. It's a great city on a high mountain with walls and gates, with foundations and streets, adorned with jewels of every kind, according to Revelation 21:9–27. Such descriptions befit a bodily resurrection.

Regarding the details of what heaven is like, however, we are going to have to wait. It will be indescribably incredible! We can anticipate heaven as being so much greater than anything we have experienced in this life. Can you imagine what being in an intimate union with God will be like? It's definitely something to look forward to.

Do only our souls go to heaven, or will our bodies go too? What will we look like in heaven? If heaven is a relationship and not a place, why do we need bodies?
St. Paul tells us that we will rise from the dead with a resurrection like Christ's:

> Do you not know that all of us who have been baptized into Christ Jesus were baptized into his death? We were buried therefore with him by baptism into death, so that as Christ was raised from the dead by the glory of the Father, we too might walk in newness of life. For if we have been united with him in a death like his, *we shall certainly be united with him in a resurrection like his.* (Romans 6:3–5; emphasis added)

Christ rose from the tomb bodily, he allowed the apostles to touch him, and he ate and drank in front of them. Since we will have "a resurrection like his," heaven will include the body. But this does not mean that our bodies in heaven will be identical to our current earthly bodies. Christ's risen body could pass through locked doors with ease, and our glorified bodies will be like his.

As human beings, we relate to others and to Christ through our bodies, which is why God gives us the sacraments, especially the Eucharist. In our new bodies we will roam the new heavens and a new earth with Christ (see Isaiah 65:17, 66:22; 2 Peter 3:13; Revelation 21:1), where "the dwelling of God is with men. He will dwell with them" (Revelation 21:3). These new heavens and earth will have plants and animals and wonderful scenic beauty. Our own bodies will appear spectacularly beautiful and not undergo pain, tiredness, illness, or suffering of any kind;

we will have complete dominion over our bodies in ways we never imagined. "[W]e await a Savior, the Lord Jesus Christ, who will change our lowly body to be like his glorious body, by the power which enables him even to subject all things to himself" (Philippians 3:20–21).

In heaven will we remember and recognize our loved ones and other people?

Our earthly and spiritual relationships are key to our identity as persons, much more than our physical appearance, accomplishments, or failures. I am who I am as God's son or daughter, as Jesus' friend and disciple, as the Holy Spirit's temple. Also, I am who I am in relationship to my parents, siblings, spouse, children (for those who have them), friends, neighbors, and coworkers.

Heaven will only strengthen our identity, by deepening the relationships we already have here on earth: "To live in heaven is 'to be with Christ.' The elect live 'in Christ' [Philippians 1:23], but they retain, or rather find, their true identity, their own name" (CCC, 1025; see Revelation 2:17).

These relationships will not disappear, but they will be purified of our selfishness. Thus, when we go to heaven we will recognize family and friends because they are an essential part of who we are. We will be able to recognize and remember every person we knew and loved on earth and interact with them.

Jesus, along with Peter, James, and John, recognized Moses and Elijah when they appeared to them in a transfigured (heavenly) form (see Matthew 17:1–13). Likewise, he describes Lazarus in the bosom of Abraham, both of whom the rich man (in torment) recognizes (see Luke 16:19–31). Much more so will it be for us in heaven.

If we have left behind some loved ones back on earth, when we die we will be able to help them even more than we did before, since we will be closer to God, in intimate union with him.

What will we do in heaven? Why doesn't God tell us more about what heaven is like?

Remember, heaven is a great family gathering, a huge wedding feast with those you love! What do you do at a wedding? In heaven we'll eat, drink, and socialize with all our friends and family. We'll dance to heavenly music and talk with people who lived long before us and long after us, even by thousands of years. It will be such a fascinating time, with many details beyond our imagination.

God doesn't tell us too much because it is meant to be a gift. Would you want your mom or dad, husband or wife, friend or family member to describe in detail the gift they bought you for your birthday? Would you want them to unwrap your present beforehand—and then rewrap it—so you could make sure it was worth inviting them to your birthday party? Let's trust that God loves us and that the gift waiting for us will be greater than we could ever imagine.

Can someone go to heaven if he or she just loves people in general, with no special relationship with Jesus Christ?

"Generic" love or goodwill toward others (benevolence) is not true love. The nature of love is very personal; it's interpersonal.

True love establishes a relationship between the lovers. Could you imagine a young man proposing to his girlfriend this way? "Mary Lou, will you marry me? I have this great generic love for all women. I couldn't imagine living without a woman; my life would simply not be complete. . . . Will you marry me?"

It's the same with God. God the Father wants us to know that he loves each of us as his very own son or daughter and wants us to treat him as our true Father. God is not satisfied with a generic love. He calls us to love him personally, to establish an intimate relationship of love between ourselves and him.

Christ also suffered and died on the cross to express the total gift of himself to each of us, inviting each one personally to respond to his gift with our own personal gift of ourselves to him. This personal relationship with him will reach fulfillment in heaven.

What about reincarnation? How does this belief fit with Christianity?

Traditionally, reincarnation is the idea that when a person dies, his spirit leaves his body and is born again as another human being or as a higher or lower animal, depending on the way that person lived his life. People who believe in reincarnation typically fear killing animals because it might mean killing some close relative, such as a parent or grandparent—although he or she would be immediately reincarnated again as something else. This belief is totally incompatible with Christianity, which believes that we die once:

> And just as it is appointed for men to die once, and after that comes judgment, so Christ, having been offered once to bear the sins of

many, will appear a second time, not to deal with sin but to save those who are eagerly waiting for him. (Hebrews 9:27–28)

Think about it. Would you really want to be reincarnated and start over, doing different things, making different mistakes, without any hope of reaching eternity? This belief really doesn't answer the quest of the human heart; it just allows us to avoid taking responsibility for our lives and to avoid facing the Absolute; it takes the focus off our relationship with God and Christ's sacrificial love on the cross. It often seems to be a response to the natural fear of death, which is very frightening to those who do not have a relationship with God.

For Christians, then, the only "reincarnation" is the resurrection of the body, which occurs when we take on an immortal and imperishable body.

How do we show Jesus that we truly love him and want to be with him forever?

Simple—the same way we develop any close relationship. First, we need to spend time with him, talking to him and listening to what he says. We regularly need to spend time in prayer and become familiar with his Word.

The more we know and love him, the more we want to serve him and carry out his commandments. In a word: Do everything you do out of love for Jesus and you will show him your love. "So, whether you eat or drink, or whatever you do, do all to the glory of God" (1 Corinthians 10:31), since "in everything God works for good [including heaven] with those who love him" (Romans 8:28).

How do you explain heaven to a child who can't understand the happiness of a bride at her wedding?

A child can understand the joy and happiness of a wedding celebration, with its hugs, smiles, and gifts. A child can also understand the joy of other family celebrations, such as a birthday or a special holiday like Christmas. There one experiences the wonderful family unity that fills everyone with joy and pleasure. In addition, there is no malice, hard feelings, hatred, or anger. All is happiness. A child can understand all this!

Can we edit or erase things on that "video"?

The video analogy represents the fact that everything we do is recorded: the good, the bad, and the ugly! And God will judge us according to our deeds:

> For he will render to every man according to his works: to those who by patience in well-doing seek for glory and honor and immortality, he will give eternal life; but for those who are factious and do not obey the truth, but obey wickedness, there will be wrath and fury. There will be tribulation and distress for every human being who does evil . . . (Romans 2:6–9)

If we bring our shameful, sinful deeds before a priest authorized by the Holy Spirit to forgive them (see John 20:22–23), then effectively those deeds will be erased from our video. This is what happens when Catholics go to confession (we will discuss this further in the chapter on sin).

How should we approach our own death?

Let's answer this by looking at how Christ approached his impending death:

> I am the good shepherd; . . . and I lay down my life for the sheep. . . . For this reason the Father loves me, because I lay down my life, that I may take it again. No one takes it from me, but I lay it down of my own accord. I have power to lay it down, and I have power to take it again . . . (John 10:14–18)

Christ saw death as a total gift of self. Such a view is very healthy, and we too should want to lay down our lives for others and give our all to Christ. But this doesn't mean we should have some kind of a death wish. Just as a bride spends much time and effort planning her wedding, wanting to make it special so she can demonstrate to the whole world how she's giving herself totally to her groom, we should view our life here on earth as a great wedding preparation. We work hard to get everything ready: inviting many guests, sharing our faith, and living with such generosity and faithfulness to Christ that everyone knows we are going to heaven with complete freedom and anticipation.

If, on the other hand, we seek death in order to be done with living on earth as soon as possible, or as a way to avoid giving of ourselves, avoiding the effort and suffering involved in preparing for our wedding (the gift of our very lives to Christ), that is a sign that we are still selfish, not ready to relinquish control of our lives to Christ. It shows that we are not really interested in heaven, or loving Christ with all our heart, mind, strength, and soul.

THREE

To Hell with Hell?

Heaven is a spiritual reality, and so is hell. Yet many find hell's existence totally unacceptable. If God is truly all-loving and all-merciful, how could he ever punish people for all eternity? If God were truly all-merciful, would he torture souls without end? Would a loving God really do this? By their reasoning, with this one fell swoop, hell has been eliminated and heaven is subsequently challenged.

Hell appears in many Bible passages: Jesus describes it as the "outer darkness," "furnace of fire," and "unquenchable fire" (see Matthew 13:42, 25:30; Mark 9:43), specifically calling it "*eternal* punishment" (Matthew 25:46; emphasis added) and "*eternal* fire" (Matthew 25:41; emphasis added). The Book of Revelation portrays hell as a "second death" and a "lake of fire" prepared for those excluded from the book of life (see Revelation 20:6–15). St. Paul describes this Christian belief as "eternal destruction" in 2 Thessalonians 1:6–9.

Some argue that hell exists in order to fulfill God's infinite justice. But would an eternal punishment be just for a temporal sin? It doesn't seem fair. Thus even God's justice is challenged in this line of thinking, because no crime, however hideous, could ever merit eternal punishment.

HELL AND GOD'S MERCY

Hell should not contradict the reality of God as all-merciful and all-loving; rather, it should actually prove it. In other words, hell would not be possible if God were not infinitely merciful and loving.

Let's think this through.

Have you ever known two people who hated each other? Usually these two individuals once had a great mutual love but for one reason or another had a falling out, perhaps accompanied by some act of disloyalty or infidelity. They drifted apart and became indifferent to each other, and then ended up hating each other. Perhaps it was a married couple whose relationship ended in a bitter divorce. Perhaps it was a boyfriend-girlfriend or parent-child relationship. It may have been a relationship between siblings, or best friends. Whatever the case, two individuals who had once loved each other ended their relationship feeling severe animosity toward each other.

Now, what happens when two people hate each other? They just can't stand being near each other. Maybe they happen to be invited to the same party—perhaps a wedding feast—which may be quite enjoyable, with great food, drink, music, and so on. Everyone is having a grand old time—except these two. When they see each other, there are fireworks! Each begins to recall old memories and old hurts, resentments start to rise up inside, and the hate starts to boil over until one of them can't stand it any longer and leaves.

Now, what happens when a person dies hating God? Wouldn't that person want to get as far away as possible from the God he or she hates? But where can you go to get away from God? He is everywhere! He is in the very depths of our being; we have been made in his image and likeness:

> Where can I go from your spirit? From your presence, where can I flee? If I ascend to the heavens, you are there; if I lie down in Sheol, there you are. If I take the wings of dawn and dwell beyond the sea, even there your hand guides me, your right hand holds me fast. If I say, "Surely darkness shall hide me, and night shall be my light"— darkness is not dark for you, and night shines as the day. Darkness and light are but one. You formed my inmost being; you knit me in my mother's womb. (Psalm 139:7–13, NAB)

A soul who hates God wants to flee as far as possible from him, from the light, as St. John puts it:

> And this is the judgment, that the light has come into the world, and men loved darkness rather than light, because their deeds were evil. For *every one who does evil hates the light*, and does not come to the light, lest his deeds should be exposed. But he who does what is true comes to the light, that it may be clearly seen that his deeds have been wrought in God. (John 3:19–21, emphasis added)

Such a soul wouldn't want to go to heaven to see the God he or she hates face-to-face in an eternal marital intimacy of Christ with his Church. No way! Instead this soul tries to flee from God, to get far away from him. But God is everywhere— where can someone go? God, in his mercy, does not force a soul to be with him in heaven. In fact, he mercifully shields that soul from his presence (see 2 Thessalonians 1:9).

SELF-INFLICTED TORTURE

So, in his mercy, God excludes from his presence the soul who dies hating him, and then he allows that soul to live for all eternity in darkness. Nevertheless, God's presence is felt even in hell. A soul in hell looks inwardly and sees the image of the God whom he hates, because every person has been made in the image and likeness of God. Even in hell, a soul can't avoid seeing reminders of God.

And what do people do when they see a picture or image of a person they hate? They try to destroy it—tear the picture up, stomp on it, spit on it, show contempt for it. Similarly, the soul in hell looks inwardly—at itself—and sees an image of God and tries to destroy it, showing utter contempt for that image. It tries to burn the image . . . cut it with swords . . . hide it in utter darkness so it can't be seen . . . cover it with vile slime so worms will infest it. In hating God, a soul tries to destroy itself in a kind of eternal suicide attempt.

Hell is the place of these horrific punishments. It's important to remember that these tortures are all self-inflicted by a soul who hates its Creator. To such a soul heaven would be far worse, because in heaven the soul "shall see him [the object of its hate] as he is" (1 John 3:2). For that soul heaven would produce even more torment because it would be in the Church's eternal marital union with the person it hates.

So, remember, God in his mercy does not force us to love him. Hell exists only because God is merciful!

HELL AND GOD'S LOVE

Many individuals contest this line of thinking: "If God were truly merciful, he would allow those souls who die hating him simply to cease to exist. That seems to be what they want anyway. Why wouldn't God just allow those souls to drop out of existence into nothingness?"

To answer that, we have to ask another question: What would God have to do for a soul to cease to exist? The answer is quite simple. All God would have to do is stop loving that soul and poof, it would cease to exist! God loved us into existence. When he thought about our possibility, he loved that thought and we came into being. Now, for us to stop existing, God would have to stop loving us.

But God's love is eternal! It never ends. Once God begins loving us, he can't stop: "The steadfast love of the LORD never ceases, his mercies never come to an end" (Lamentations 3:22). God continues to love us even if we reject that love: "Can a woman forget her sucking child, that she should have no compassion on the son of her womb? Even these may forget, yet I will not forget you" (Isaiah 49:15).

That's why hell could exist only if God is truly all-loving and all-merciful. Love and mercy do not go against God's justice, because all hell's tortures are self-inflicted by souls who have rejected God's love.

God invites us all to the wedding feast, as Jesus describes in Luke 14:15–24. Yet some choose hell by choosing not to go to the feast. One chooses to go out and see his field, putting his material possessions ahead of God. Still others put their human relationships ahead of God. Only those who choose God over everything else enter the wedding feast. No one is forced to go to hell, just like no one is forced to go to heaven. That's why Jesus calls the damned not *condemned* but simply *cursed* (see Matthew 25:41)—neither Christ nor his Father condemns anyone to hell; those who go to hell condemn themselves (see John 3:16–21).

Pope Benedict XVI wrote:

> But God never forgets, and we all continue in being because he loves us and because his thinking of us is creative and gives us existence. Our eternity is based on his love. Anyone whom God loves never ceases to be. In him, in his thinking and loving, it is not just a shadow of us that continues in being; rather, in him and his creative love we ourselves, with all that we are and all that is most ourselves, are preserved immortally and forever in being. It is his love that makes us immortal. This love guarantees our immortality.[4]

Hell is real. It is the fruit not of God's wrath, but of his love and mercy. We don't avoid hell by avoiding God's anger but by accepting his mercy and embracing his love.

QUESTIONS AND ANSWERS

If God is love—not a judging tyrant—how could he allow anyone to choose hell?

God *is* love, but he does not force anyone to love him back. Painfully, he respects the freedom that he has given us, even when our free choices hurt us and others.

God "desires all men to be saved and to come to the

knowledge of the truth" (1 Timothy 2:4); he wants us all to be with him in heaven. However, some don't want to be in heaven; they reject his love and the salvation that he has won for them. They *choose* hell, as a way to flee from the light: "For every one who does evil hates the light, and does not come to the light, lest his deeds should be exposed" (John 3:20).

We can't accuse God of being a tyrant, because we choose to flee from him.

If God forgives all our sins, why do people go to hell?

For God to forgive us, we first have to acknowledge our sins and ask for forgiveness. However, if we don't acknowledge that we have freely chosen to be selfish, proud, uncaring, mean, and so on, and instead we blame God or others for the damage and hurt that we have caused, then we don't give God an opportunity to forgive us.

This is what happens with the souls in hell. They don't want God's forgiveness. They are angry with God, and they blame him for all their misery. They choose to flee from his presence and seek some kind of morbid consolation in self-torture.

Where is hell? Is it really made of fire and brimstone? Does it last for all eternity?

We can think of hell as a kind of eternal suicide attempt—the Book of Revelation calls it a second death—in which a soul can't ever finish killing itself off. Although hell will be in some physical location (since the souls in hell will have their bodies), it's more a state of fleeing God's presence. Exactly where hell is located is a mystery reserved only for God to know.

Dante's _Inferno_ gives a different spot in hell for each type of sin. Is that true?

Dante's _Inferno_ is not Sacred Scripture; it's a fictional depiction of hell as the author imagined it. He tried to show how people with different kinds of sins might suffer differently. Again, this goes along with the tortures of hell being self-inflicted.

Does the devil torture souls in hell? If hell is this place of self-torture where souls seek self-destruction, then what place does the devil have there?

Souls in hell seek to destroy the image and likeness of God that they see and hate in themselves. Satan and his minions also hate God's image and likeness, and they are quite willing to help those souls inflict horrible tortures upon themselves. They do everything they can to help them destroy God's image.

So, demons fit this self-inflicted torture scenario of hell quite well.

Can someone really hate God?

God gives us free will. He loves us and desires us to love him back. He invites us to enter into a relationship with him, but he respects our freedom. We are free to reject that invitation; we are free to reject his love. A person can hate God just like a person can hate a father or mother; it's unnatural, but unfortunately it happens.

Jean-Paul Sartre described his own relationship with God in these haunting words: "I felt the presence of God only once, and flew into such a rage . . . whirled about . . . blasphemed . . . [until] He never looked at me again."[5]

Pope Benedict XVI also describes this possibility:

> With death, our life-choice becomes definitive—our life stands before the judge. Our choice, which in the course of an entire life takes on a certain shape, can have a variety of forms. There can be people who have totally destroyed their desire for truth and readiness to love, people for whom everything has become a lie, people who have lived for hatred and have suppressed all love within themselves. This is a terrifying thought, but alarming profiles of this type can be seen in certain figures of our own history. In such people all would be beyond remedy and the destruction of good would be irrevocable: this is what we mean by the word *Hell*. (*Spe Salvi*, 45)

What if I don't hate God—could I still go to hell?

Remember what we said in the previous chapter on heaven. There, it was clear that we express our love for God by entering into the Church's union with Christ. Our life is an opportunity for us to fall in love and to show God that we love him. As Jesus said: "He who loves father or mother more than me is not worthy of me; and he who loves son or daughter more than me is not worthy of me; and he who does not take his cross and follow me is not worthy of me" (Matthew 10:38–39).

God calls us to love him above all persons and things. However, if a person lived his whole life as though God did not exist, would he want to go to heaven? Jesus gives us a wonderfully detailed parable in Matthew 25:14–30:

> "For [the kingdom of heaven] will be as when a man going on a journey called his servants and entrusted to them his property; to

one he gave five talents, to another two, to another one, to each according to his ability. Then he went away. He who had received the five talents went at once and traded with them; and he made five talents more. . . . But he who had received the one talent went and dug in the ground and hid his master's money. Now after a long time the master of those servants came and settled accounts with them. And he who had received the five talents came forward, bringing five talents more, saying, 'Master, you delivered to me five talents; here I have made five talents more.' His master said to him, 'Well done, good and faithful servant; you have been faithful over a little, I will set you over much; enter into the joy of your master.' . . . He also who had received the one talent came forward, saying, 'Master, I knew you to be a hard man, reaping where you did not sow, and gathering where you did not winnow; so I was afraid, and I went and hid your talent in the ground. Here you have what is yours.' But his master answered him, 'You wicked and slothful servant! You knew that I reap where I have not sowed, and gather where I have not winnowed? Then you ought to have invested my money with the bankers, and at my coming I should have received what was my own with interest.' . . . And [he] cast the worthless servant into the outer darkness; there men will weep and gnash their teeth.'"

The man with one talent lived his whole life as though God— the Master—did not exist. He didn't steal, murder, or rape anyone; he simply buried his talent in the ground and left it there, and then lived his life as though he didn't have it. When it came time to render an account of his life, he was sent to hell, where he could best continue living his life as though God did not exist.

If a soul dies after living a selfish life, he can very easily blame God for not fulfilling all his desires. He may react like a spoiled child who blames his parents for not giving him what he wants and screams at them, "I hate you!" Instead, let's strive to live in such a way that we would never be tempted to react that way toward our beloved Father, God.

Do I have to pray to go to heaven? I just don't have time. Would you want to spend a lot of time with someone who never spoke to you or had time for you? Hardly. If you want to spend the rest of eternity with God, you should look for opportunities to spend time with him, trying to express your love for him and seeking to have special moments alone with him. In this way you begin to show him now what attitude you intend to have for eternity: one of being close to him and communing with him.

When the great king—God—invited guests to the wedding feast, those invited came up with all sorts of excuses: too busy inspecting his new field (new work), too busy with his new oxen (new automobile) or with his new wife (see Luke 14:15–24). These are all good things—but they are no substitute for prayer and a deep personal relationship with God.

In 1 John 5:13 we read that if we believe in Jesus, we know we have eternal life. Should believers ever be concerned about hell? Wouldn't that show a lack of true faith?

Those who believe in Jesus Christ become his disciples and friends. At the Last Supper he told his disciples: "No longer do I call you servants, for the servant does not know what his master is doing; but I have called you friends, for all that I have heard from my Father I have made known to you" (John 15:15). But Jesus also wanted his friends to be aware of hell as they carried out their mission: "I tell you, *my friends,* do not fear those who kill the body, and after that have no more that they can do. But I will warn you whom to fear: fear him who, after he has killed, has power to cast into hell; yes, I tell you, fear him!" (Luke 12:4–5; emphasis added). Hell should be feared by all, even by believers—even by Christ's *friends*! A healthy fear will help us to avoid temptation and keep us focused on carrying out the good works that God calls us to do.

FOUR

Sin Is Hell

Some think we reach heaven by default: "If I don't commit any really big sin, then why would God deny me heaven and send me to hell?" But, using the marriage analogy again, let's imagine a young man approaching a pretty girl and saying, "Sally, will you marry me? I've never done anything really bad to you. I've never spit in your face, tripped you on the sidewalk, or called you names. So, will you marry me?" Of course, she'd say, "No way! I'm going to marry someone who loves me . . . and someone I love."

This young woman won't marry someone just because he says he loves her; even less would she do so if he treated her badly. Sin is simply contrary to love. If we truly loved Jesus Christ and wanted to spend eternity with him, we would naturally love him, and we would strive to remain pure and blameless—sinless—as a way to show him our love. As St. Paul describes it:

It is my prayer that your love may abound more and more, with knowledge and all discernment, so that you may approve what is excellent, and may be pure and blameless for the day of Christ, filled with the fruits of righteousness which come through Jesus Christ, to the glory and praise of God. (Philippians 1:9–11)

Love makes us ready for the Judgment Day, when we will make our definitive choice: to come to the light of heaven or to flee to the darkness (see John 3:19–21). Our current choices— to love God and grow in virtue, or to sin—are linked to our definitive choice at the end of our lives.

But if God is merciful, won't he forgive all our sins on the Judgment Day? To have salvation dependent on our choices seems to mean that we must *earn* heaven—that it's not God's free and gratuitous gift of grace.

Let's plumb the Scripture a bit more on this.

DOES ANYONE SIN ANYMORE?

Before Adam and Eve sinned, life was good. They were made in the image and likeness of God, they walked with him, and they had complete control of their humanity. They were naked but felt no shame. But death, illness, and shame entered the world with their sin.

Central to the message of Jesus Christ is that he suffered and died on the cross to save us from the eternal punishment resulting from our sins. However, these days few people think they have sinned; we have lost the sense of sin.[6] We objectify sin and then discard it. We dismiss our sin by rationalizing it away. We use a cost-benefit analysis on our actions, thinking,

"If I don't hurt anybody, then how can it be a sin? If it's an act between consenting adults, then how can it be a sin?" In modern times, to be considered a sinner, one must be a truly evil person—Hitler, Stalin, a serial killer, a terrorist, or a rapist.

Another way we dismiss sin is by trying to find a genetic cause for every kind of action—violent behavior, homosexual or deviant sexual behavior, irresponsibility, and so on. It's as though we are determined to find the "sin gene" in order to relieve ourselves of any moral responsibility. You see, if we can define sin biologically, we eradicate our responsibility to behave and can then blame a certain "predisposition" for that behavior, so that it's no longer a choice but some base animal instinct.

CATHOLIC GUILT AND RULES

Some people view the Catholic approach to sin as blindly following rules: If you follow the rules, then you go to heaven; if you disregard the rules, then you go to hell. Heaven and hell become the carrot and the stick to get people to follow arbitrary rules imposed upon them by those in power—that is, the Church's hierarchy.

Consider, for example, the rule for going to Mass on Sunday. The Church teaches that to *deliberately* miss a Sunday Mass—because of laziness, a desire to watch football, or some other superficial reason—is a mortal sin.[7] If such a sin goes unrepented, it will cause the culprit to forfeit heaven and go to hell. Using our modern culture's analysis, however, the question becomes: "How could it be a sin, since I haven't hurt anybody?" and the rationalizations follow:

"I can pray better at home, and I don't get anything out of Mass anyway."

"I find it boring, and the sermon is irrelevant to what's going on in my life."

"I prefer to worship God in nature."

The cost-benefit analysis concludes: "Missing Mass cannot be wrong because I benefit so much more from not going."

But put this in the context of a relationship. If a young man were to say to his girlfriend, "Honey, I love you a lot. You and I have a very special relationship, beyond any other couple I know. But let's face it, you're a very busy woman—with your demanding job, all your social commitments, and your hobbies—and I'm a very busy guy. Why don't we just plan on seeing each other, say, once a month or so? Is that okay?"

How would his girlfriend react to this? She'd be very upset, wouldn't she? Although he's saying with his lips, "I love you," his suggesting "giving each other space" and not seeing each other much is telling her that she's really not that important to him. It would kill the relationship! So too when a Catholic misses a very important "date" with God on Sunday: Although she may say with her lips that she loves him, her action of staying in bed or watching a ball game instead reveals that Christ is not that important to her. It could kill her relationship with Jesus!

Once I was trying to convey the importance of attending Sunday Mass to a young man who was not easily convinced; he kept throwing out objections. Finally he said to me, "But why should I go to Mass on Sunday if I don't get anything out of it?"

I asked him if he had a girlfriend; he said he did. Then I asked him if he ever showed affection to her, perhaps spontaneously reaching for her hand as they walked along, without getting anything out of it. Slamming his hand on the table, he exclaimed: "That's not fair!" He knew immediately that there were many occasions that he "had" to treat his girlfriend with affection, not because he was going to get something out of it, but because not showing her affection would hurt their relationship and could even cause a fight that would end it all.

The key to understanding sin is to see how our actions impact our relationship with God. God does not impose the commandments as arbitrary rules to control us. Rather, the commandments are manifestations of his love, showing us how our actions impact our relationship with him. Sin separates us from God and puts distance between us. He gives us the commandments only because he loves us and wants us to know how to love him in return:

> "If you love me, you will keep my commandments. . . . He who has my commandments and keeps them, he it is who loves me; and he who loves me will be loved by my Father, and I will love him and manifest myself to him." (John 14:15, 21)

ARE IMPURE THOUGHTS SINFUL?

Another criticism of Christians deals with sexual morality. Critics say, "You Christians are so puritanical about sex. You even think that impure thoughts or looks are sinful—mortally sinful, at that. How ridiculous—how can thoughts hurt anyone?" And regarding the sin of looking at naked bodies, they ask, "Why would God make the human body so beautiful if he didn't want us to look?"

First, it was Jesus Christ who called impure thoughts and looks sinful:

"You have heard that it was said, 'You shall not commit adultery.' But I say to you that every one who looks at a woman lustfully has already committed adultery with her in his heart. If your right eye causes you to sin, pluck it out and throw it away; it is better that you lose one of your members than that your whole body be thrown into hell. And if your right hand causes you to sin, cut it off and throw it away; it is better that you lose one of your members than that your whole body go into hell." (Matthew 5:27–30)

Looking lustfully at someone's body is adultery of the heart, which was a capital offense in the Old Testament, punishable by stoning—a *mortal* sin. Thus, Jesus equated lustful looks with adultery: One could lose one's life—one's relationship with God—just for looking lustfully at a woman in one's heart, even though he didn't "hurt" anybody.

Here again, this makes perfect sense in the context of a relationship. Suppose we see a young woman and a young man walking down the street together, holding hands and having a great time together, obviously in love. And as they are walking together, an immodestly dressed woman passes by, and the young man, weak as he is, starts stealing some glances at the woman; then his eyes latch on to her, and he turns his head, and . . . bang! He runs into a telephone pole.

Now, how would this man's girlfriend react? She'd be livid! The young man tells her, "Hey, honey, you shouldn't be upset. I didn't do anything to hurt you. I'm the one who got hurt—I've got this big bump on my forehead for being so stupid. But you shouldn't feel hurt."

But she *is* hurt—and justifiably so—for he was unfaithful to her with his eyes. He basically said to his girlfriend, with his choice and his actions, "Honey, guess what? You've got competition, and you happen to be losing to that competition right now."

What do we say to God when we entertain our impure thoughts by "looking" at them? "Hey, Lord, you've got competition, and you happen to be losing that competition right now." It's not a very pleasant statement to make to someone we are called to love with our whole heart, mind, strength, and soul.

This is why God expressed idolatry as a form of adultery; he wanted the people of Israel to understand how this sin hurt their relationship with him. He even sent the prophet Nathan to David to show how his sin—adultery with Bathsheba and killing her husband in battle—killed his relationship with God. Nathan's parable helped David open his eyes to see his guilt (see 2 Samuel 11:1–12:15).

EYES ONLY FOR YOU!

This does not mean that Christian morality is principally negative, focused exclusively on avoiding sinful acts and thoughts. Christian morality is radically positive. It's about love—that is, affirming our relationships of love with our thoughts, words, and actions. We can understand right and wrong, heaven and hell, and all salvation history only in the context of love.

Let's return to our example and transform it into a positive one: We see the young woman and man—girlfriend and boyfriend—walking down the street together, holding hands and having a great time. Again, as they walk, an immodestly dressed woman passes by. But this time, the young man intentionally doesn't look. Perhaps he turns and looks into his girlfriend's eyes instead.

Now, how would this man's girlfriend react? "Wow! He really loves me. He only has eyes for me. He only has a heart for me." The act of not looking says more than a hundred "I love yous."

The same happens in our relationship with Jesus. Our not "looking" at temptations that pop into our imagination tells him, "I really love you. I only have eyes for you. I only have a heart for you." The act of not looking says more than hundreds of "I love yous" would.

It comes down to this: Everything we do has meaning for our relationship with God. Everything we do can express our love or our selfishness. This includes other actions or inactions on our part, as Jesus reminds us: "As you did it to one of the least of these my brethren, you did to me" (Matthew 25:40). Any attitudes and actions we take toward others become attitudes and actions toward Christ. All parents understand this, because when someone treats one of their children unfairly, *they* feel mistreated; when their children are praised, *they* feel praised.

Thus, our sins are actions that negatively impact our relationship with God. That's what makes a sin a sin.

CONFESS YOUR SINS

Fortunately there is a remedy for our sin: confessing it to our advocate, Jesus Christ.

If we say we have no sin, we deceive ourselves, and the truth is not in us. If we confess our sins, he is faithful and just, and will forgive our sins and cleanse us from all unrighteousness. If we say we have not sinned, we make him a liar, and his word is not in us. . . . [B]ut if any one does sin, we have an advocate with the Father, Jesus Christ the righteous; and he is the expiation for our sins, and not for ours only but also for the sins of the whole world. (1 John 1:8–2:2)

In the Old Testament, if a person sinned inadvertently against the law, he would confess his sin to a priest. The priest would instruct the person on what sacrifice was needed; the person would bring a bull, goat, or some other animal, the priest would sacrifice the sin offering, and the person's sin would be forgiven. Various such sin offerings are described in the Book of Leviticus, always ending in the priests making atonement and with the declaration that the person's sins "shall be forgiven." Likewise, after Solomon finished the Temple of God's special presence, the people of Israel went to the Temple and confessed their sins to the priest. Then God forgave their sins (see 1 Kings 8:31–53; 2 Chronicles 6:22–39; 7:12–15).

Yet these were just a foreshadowing of the single sacrifice made for our sins by Christ, who, after rising from the dead, appointed apostles and gave them power from the Holy Spirit:

On the evening of that day, the first day of the week, the doors being shut where the disciples were, for fear of the Jews, Jesus came and stood among them and said to them, "Peace be with you." When he had said this, he showed them his hands and his side. Then the disciples were glad when they saw the Lord. Jesus . . . breathed on them, and said to them, "Receive the Holy Spirit. If you forgive the sins of any, they are forgiven; if you retain the sins of any, they are retained." (John 20:19–23)

The Holy Spirit empowered these apostle-priests to apply the one sin offering of Christ on the cross, and our sins are forgiven. Wow! God actually forgives our sins through Christ's priests—channels of God's grace and forgiveness! That's why we go to confession.

HE BECAME SIN

To really understand how serious our sins are, consider Christ's suffering on the cross. Contemplating the cross, St. Paul realized that Christ, who "knew no sin," became sin for us so we could become "the righteousness of God" (2 Corinthians 5:21). He bore our sins in his body on the cross so we could be healed and freed from the bondage of sin.

Sin alienates us and separates us from God; thus, sin is hell. Sin not only causes death, it is death—and second death is hell (see Revelation 2:11, 20:6–14).

Jesus' identification with our sin was so great that he too experienced sin's alienation from his heavenly Father. He expressed this sense of complete alienation with his shocking cry from the cross:

And when the sixth hour had come, there was darkness over the whole land until the ninth hour. And at the ninth hour Jesus cried with a loud voice, "Eloi, Eloi, lama sabach-thani?" which means, "My God, my God, why hast thou forsaken me?" (Mark 15:33–34)

In his humanity Jesus felt forsaken by and separated from his Father, because he took our sin upon himself. Yet he still confidently addressed his heavenly Father from the cross as *Father* when he said, "Father, forgive them; for they know not what they do" (Luke 23:34); and before breathing his last, "Father, into thy hands I commit my spirit!" (Luke 23:46). Christ maintained a great intimacy with his heavenly Father while experiencing the most complete alienation possible, the alienation of our sins. He truly experienced hell on earth.

QUESTIONS AND ANSWERS

Will I go to hell if I accept Jesus Christ as my Lord and Savior but continue to sin?

It's not enough to say you love God with words; you need to give him all that you have and all that you are, and that involves fighting against sin. That's why St. John says:

> Every one who commits sin is guilty of lawlessness; sin is lawlessness. You know that he appeared to take away sins, and in him there is no sin. No one who abides in him sins; no one who sins has either seen him or known him. . . . He who commits sin is of the devil; for the devil has sinned from the beginning. The reason the Son of God appeared was to destroy the works of the devil. No one born of God commits sin; for God's nature abides in him, and he cannot sin because he is born of God. (1 John 3:4–9)

Let's trust in God's mercy and abide in him, which is heaven. Not to abide in God is sin—it's hell.

Sin is sin, right? So why do Catholics have different levels of sin, such as mortal and venial sins?

St. John contrasted "mortal" sin and "sin that is not mortal":

> I write this to you who believe in the name of the Son of God, that you may know that you have eternal life. . . . If any one sees his brother committing what is not a mortal sin, he will ask, and God will give him life for those whose sin is not mortal. There is sin which is mortal; I do not say that one is to pray for that. All wrongdoing is sin, but there is sin which is not mortal. (1 John 5:13–17)

The Old Testament prefigures this description, defining various sins as mortal or capital (for which a person would lose his or her life). These included murder, sexual sins (harlotry, rape, adultery, homosexuality, and bestiality), blasphemy, and defiling the sacred. St. Paul links mortal sin to the loss of heaven:

> Now the works of the flesh are plain: immorality, impurity, licentiousness, idolatry, sorcery, enmity, strife, jealousy, anger, selfishness, dissension, party spirit, envy, drunkenness, carousing, and the like. I warn you, as I warned you before, that those who do such things shall not inherit the kingdom of God. (Galatians 5:19–21)

In the Bible the concept of deadly sin is quite prevalent, if not fully developed.

Is there any sin that can't be forgiven?

Jesus mentions one unforgivable sin—blasphemy against the Holy Spirit:

"Truly, I say to you, all sins will be forgiven the sons of men, and whatever blasphemies they utter; but whoever blasphemes against the Holy Spirit never has forgiveness, but is guilty of an eternal sin"—for they had said, "He has an unclean spirit." (Mark 3:28–30)

Jewish leaders committed blasphemy against the Holy Spirit—the unforgivable sin—when they rejected their authority to discern who Jesus was (the Messiah) and instead accused him of casting out demons "by Beelzebul, the prince of demons" (Matthew 12:22–28). Using their Spirit-given authority to oppose—rather than to affirm—the Spirit's teaching is the sin against the Holy Spirit. That's why Jesus cursed them: "Woe to you, scribes and Pharisees, hypocrites! because you shut the kingdom of heaven against men; for you neither enter yourselves, nor allow those who would enter to go in" (Matthew 23:13).

If you are gay, can you go to heaven?

One day the scribes and Pharisees brought Jesus a woman who had been caught in the act of adultery. They asked him what he would do with her, because the Old Testament law required her to be stoned. Jesus, however, didn't give them the answer they expected. Instead he said, "Let him who is without sin among you be the first to throw a stone at her" (John 8:7).

And look how he responded to the woman herself, after her accusers walked away: "Jesus looked up and said to her, 'Woman, where are they? Has no one condemned you?' She said, 'No one, Lord.' And Jesus said, 'Neither do I condemn you; go, and do not sin again'" (John 8:10–11).

Need we say more? Just as someone who commits adultery, someone who is actively gay but repents and tries not to sin again will receive God's mercy. Those who have same-sex attraction but who strive to keep their eyes and heart focused only on Jesus will give a wonderful witness to others and will please him.

Why can't I just confess my sins directly to God?

You can and you should. In fact, when we become aware that we have done something to hurt our relationship with Christ, the Catholic Church encourages us to acknowledge our sin and pray for pardon—but then go to confession as soon as possible. It's not an *either-or* but a *both-and* recommendation.

Again, think of a relationship. Suppose your father rashly accuses you of something you didn't do. He humiliates you in front of your friends without hearing your side of the story. Later that night, when you are asleep, he discovers his error. Getting up early in the morning, he writes you a note of apology and slips it under your door before you wake up.

Would you appreciate his apology? Sure! But would you prefer a written note of apology or the more difficult and demanding oral apology in which he speaks to you face-to-face and risks that you may not be ready to forgive and may even voice your anger and hurt? Most people would prefer to receive the more difficult and personal apology face-to-face. We do this with God by going to confession. Sure, it's more difficult, but it's also more reassuring when we hear Christ's words of forgiving love: "and your sins are forgiven."

St. Josemaría Escrivá connected confession with entering into our eternal relationship with Christ:

God is waiting for many people to take a good bath in the Sacrament of Penance! And he has a great feast ready for them, the wedding feast, the banquet of the Eucharist: the wedding-ring of the covenant, of faithfulness and never-ending friendship. May many people go to confession. . . . May there be many who approach the forgiveness of God![8]

Isn't confessing to a priest really just confessing to a human being?

Catholics see the priest as a man who has been set apart, someone who "is appointed to act on behalf of men in relation to God" (Hebrews 5:1). Jesus first gave this role to his apostles, telling them, "He who hears you hears me, and he who rejects you rejects me, and he who rejects me rejects him who sent me" (Luke 10:16). Thus if they "forgive the sins of any, they are forgiven" (John 20:23), even though only God can forgive sins (see Mark 2:7).

It is God who forgives our sins, through his ambassadors, who appeal on Christ's behalf to reconcile us with God. This is their God-given "ministry of reconciliation" (2 Corinthians 5:18). Nathan was God's ambassador to make David aware of the sinfulness of his fornication with Bathsheba and his murdering Uriah (2 Samuel 11–12). God even sent St. Paul to correct St. Peter at one point. Scripture makes it clear that God uses human beings to help us be accountable for our sins.

Do I have to go to confession?

Do you have to take a shower? Do you have to brush your teeth? No, you don't "have to" in the absolute sense. Certainly there are examples of people in the Bible who didn't go to confession.

Likely they didn't take showers or brush their teeth either; at least we don't see that in the Bible.

But would I recommend that you avoid showering or brushing your teeth? No. It's important to take care of our physical hygiene, and our spiritual hygiene is even more important. We are called to holiness. The more we can take responsibility for our past life and begin anew, the more we will accomplish our goal to be united with Christ.

The *Catechism of the Catholic Church* is specific about our obligation to go to confession:

> According to the Church's command, "after having attained the age of discretion, each of the faithful is bound by an obligation faithfully to confess serious sins at least once a year." Anyone who is aware of having committed a mortal sin must not receive Holy Communion, even if he experiences deep contrition, without having first received sacramental absolution, unless he has a grave reason for receiving Communion and there is no possibility of going to confession. Children must go to the sacrament of Penance before receiving Holy Communion for the first time. (*CCC,* 1457)

Can non-Catholic Christians go to confession?

Once I heard confessions in a church next to a public high school. A young Protestant woman came into the church to pray. Seeing people go in and come out of the confessional, she felt moved to do the same.

Although I explained to her that I could not give her the Catholic sacrament, she wanted to tell me her struggles and sins. I gave her a blessing, instead of the sacramental absolution, and she was filled with peace.

Some Protestant churches do practice a form of confessing their sins "to one another" (James 5:16), because it pleases God and helps individuals repent and take responsibility for bad decisions they have made.

FIVE

Am I Really Ready for Heaven?

Scripture is a unified whole, often presenting the truth to us gradually, in bits and pieces. God wants us to ponder those pieces and put them together like a puzzle until the full, unified picture is formed.

For example, Scripture teaches us that there is only one God (see 1 Timothy 2:5), but that's only one piece—although an extremely important one—of the scriptural portrait of God. Scripture also proclaims that Jesus Christ, the Word of God, is God and with God (see John 1:1–3). From this Christians develop the whole doctrinal picture of the Trinity and the Incarnation.

Heresies arise when we exclude pieces of the whole—for example, by denying that there is only one God. Another heresy goes the other way, affirming that there is only one God but denying that Jesus is God. But neither gives us the full picture of God.

The same is true regarding heaven. So let's uncover the full picture that Scripture reveals.

AM I REALLY READY?

We saw that we cannot go to heaven if we die hating God—we just wouldn't want to. But if we don't hate God, does that mean we're ready for heaven?

God has ransomed us from sin with Christ's bloodshed for us, offering "for all time a single sacrifice for sins" (Hebrews 10:12). Because of Christ's sacrifice, God remembers our sins and misdeeds no more. This seems to say that we should go straight to heaven if we don't reject Christ when we die. But what if we have un-forgiveness in our hearts? Will we go to heaven? Would we want to?

Suppose you died and St. Peter was leading you up to the pearly gates when suddenly you noticed that someone you utterly detested was already in heaven. Would you want to enter? Perhaps this person had greatly hurt you or one of your loved ones and was now having a very intimate conversation with Jesus. Would this affect your desire for heaven? I think most would prefer not to enter. Perhaps you would even begin to hate God for being so merciful toward the person who wronged you so terribly.

Look at the prodigal son's elder brother (see Luke 15:25–32). When the prodigal son returns from his sinful foray, his father receives him back and throws a great celebration; this is an image of heaven. The elder brother comes home from working in the field—an image of the end of his earthly life—and refuses to join the party because he feels resentful toward his younger brother. Instead of enjoying the celebration, he is envious of the undeserved attention his brother receives.

Similarly, heaven would be unappealing if we had deep-seated resentments toward another person. We simply wouldn't enjoy it, as we usually hate someone who loves those we hate. All hatred, animosity, resentment, or aversion for another—God or neighbor—is an obstacle to heaven. Although God is willing to forgive our sins—no matter how serious, because Christ's blood has been shed—we wouldn't want to join him in heaven.

In addition, would God let us into heaven if someone hated us? If we had hurt another person so much that he or she would be repulsed at joining us in heaven, would God allow us to be a stumbling block for others? No. God just couldn't let someone in heaven if it would prevent others from wanting to go.

The fact is that unhealthy and unhealed earthly relationships impede our eternal rest and happiness.

WORKING OUT DIFFERENCES, SETTLING ACCOUNTS, RESOLVING UNRESOLVED INJURY

To receive divine forgiveness, we must forgive others. As Christ teaches in the Lord's Prayer: "Our Father who art in heaven . . . forgive us our debts, as we also have forgiven our debtors" (Matthew 6:9, 12). Forgiving one another unites us to each other in Christ's body to be able to join him in heavenly intimacy. We are not ready if we hold on to hurts and resentments. That's why anger and name-calling are a kind of spiritual murder, because they kill this communion: ". . . every one who is angry with his brother shall be liable to judgment; whoever insults his brother shall be liable to the council, and whoever says, 'You fool!' shall be liable to the hell of fire" (Matthew 5:22).

Few of us go through life without getting angry at or insulting a loved one, let alone an enemy. Most have said things much worse than "You fool!" to others. Very few spouses make it through marriage without insulting each other, even after accepting Jesus Christ into their lives. Such behavior makes us "liable to the hell of fire." Ouch! Yet Jesus gives us a way out of this quandary—we can reconcile ourselves with the one we have hurt:

> So if you are offering your gift at the altar, and there remember that your brother has something against you, leave your gift there before the altar and go; first be reconciled to your brother, and then come and offer your gift. (Matthew 5:23–24)

Not only should we be reconciled with our brother before being united to Jesus in the Eucharist, we need to do this before offering the gift of our whole life to him at the heavenly altar. This means that before we die, we must reconcile with everyone we have hurt, whether with our words or with our actions. Some of these people are right beside us, within our family or among our acquaintances. Let's approach them and apologize while we have the chance.

If those we've hurt are beyond our reach and we can no longer contact them—such as people to whom we may have dealt drugs, past sexual partners, etc.—let's pray for them and ask God to heal any hurt or injury we may have caused. Perhaps we can make up for this hurt by getting involved in a charitable program to help the kinds of people we have harmed—those addicted to drugs, those dying of AIDS, etc. Many women who have had an abortion have found great peace by encouraging young pregnant women to carry their children to term; thus the death of one child serves to save the lives of many others.

What happens if we die and go before the altar in heaven to offer our gift to the Almighty, and then realize that one of our brothers has something against us? At this point, we have no choice but to go before the Judge, Jesus Christ. We will be handed over to the guard (the angels), who put us in prison temporarily— that is, until the last penny is paid, or the last hurt is healed. Only then will we be free to go to heaven with our brother. This is what Catholics call purgatory, the temporary state for those who die still needing to work out their differences with others.

We must resolve all hate and hurt feelings. Even if we have lived a "good" life—like the prodigal son's elder brother—any envy, hurt, or resentment pits us against our heavenly Father, who loves our sinful younger brother too. To the elder brother this may seem unfair. But to enjoy heaven, we must let go of all envy, hurt, and resentment either in this age—the preferred moment—or in the age to come (see Matthew 12:31–32). Only mercy will triumph over judgment.

Let's imitate our good older brother, Jesus, who forgave his accusers before dying: "Father, forgive them; for they know not what they do" (Luke 23:34). Stephen did—as did other early Christians—by forgiving his persecutors as he left this world for the next: "And as they were stoning Stephen, he prayed, 'Lord Jesus, receive my spirit.' And he knelt down and cried with a loud voice, 'Lord, do not hold this sin against them.' And when he had said this, he fell asleep" (Acts 7:59–60). This confirms what Jesus taught us: to pray for God to forgive us our sins *as we forgive those who have hurt us.*

A "BLANK CHECK" TO HEAVEN

When someone hurts us, we tend to focus on ourselves, on *our* hurt, on how *our* dreams have been ruined and how *our* lives are worse afterward. Often we feel sorry for ourselves, playing the role of the victim, expecting everyone to come to our aid.

But in reality, we should thank the person who harmed us. This individual has done us a great service because he or she has given us a "blank check" to heaven. First we must take the focus off ourselves and our hurt and focus on God. Then we can see how this person has given us a wonderful opportunity to forgive; if we do forgive, God will also forgive us.

> "Be merciful, even as your Father is merciful. Judge not, and you will not be judged; condemn not, and you will not be condemned; forgive, and you will be forgiven; give, and it will be given to you; ... For the measure you give will be the measure you get back." (Luke 6:36–38)

If we can forgive the "unforgivable" offense against us, then God will forgive us. If we refuse to judge others, then God is bound not to judge us. But a quick ticket to hell is an unforgiving heart. Jesus told the story of a servant who owed the king a large debt that he couldn't pay. The king ordered him to be sold, along with his wife and children and all his possessions, in order to pay what he owed. The man begged the king for mercy, and the king took pity on him and forgave his debt. But then this same servant saw one of his fellow servants, who owed him a much smaller amount, and demanded that he pay up. His colleague asked for patience, promising to pay when he could, but instead the servant had him thrown into prison. When the other servants saw what had happened, they went to the king and told him about it. The king called for the first servant, saying, "You wicked servant! I forgave you all that debt because you besought me; and should not you have had mercy on your fellow servant, as I had mercy on you?" (Matthew 18:32–33). And the king angrily had the servant imprisoned until he could pay his much larger debt. Jesus finished by saying, "So also my heavenly Father will do to every one of you, if you do not forgive your brother from your heart" (Matthew 18:35).

Although our anger and hurt may blind us, what other people owe us is insignificant compared to what we owe God. And we can easily overcome the debt we owe God by forgiving others. It's truly amazing when those who have been abused forgive and let go of their past hurt and anger. They can then thank God for his love and mercy.[9] Or when the family of a murder victim forgives the murderer for robbing a loved one of life, its members often experience great peace and healing.

Regarding those who die without having forgiven those who have hurt them, we hope in God's merciful love and that he will give them the opportunity to let go and be purged and purified of their hurt. He wants them to enter the joyful celebration with their prodigal brother—and with him, their heavenly Father.

Would a soul who retains anger, hurt, pain, and hate toward its abuser or murderer really want to enter heaven? In heaven, that soul would see reformed and repentant abusers or murderers— even if its own victimizer were to go to hell. Wouldn't such souls want to get away from those reminders?

We cannot go to heaven if we still hate anyone: "He who says he is in the light and hates his brother is in the darkness still" (1 John 2:9). But what we can do is forgive as best we can. Forgiving others is purification. It's the belief that all things—

good or bad—work "for good with those who love him" (Romans 8:28), so we may have fellowship with the Father, Son, and Holy Spirit, and with one another.

WHAT HAPPENS IF WE DIE WITHOUT FORGIVING SOMEONE?

The passages we've looked at in this chapter describe how God requires us to forgive, to let go of resentment—"either in this age or in the age to come" (Matthew 12:32). Catholics give this a name; we call it *purgatory*. Even though the Bible doesn't mention the word *purgatory* explicitly, it is simply a place or state of purification. This purification takes place when we participate in Christ's suffering on the cross.

The good thief is a wonderful example. He was on his cross next to Christ when everyone was taunting him; even the other thief joined in the mockery with the scribes and priests. Yet this thief defended Jesus:

> One of the criminals who were hanged railed at him, saying, "Are you not the Christ? Save yourself and us!" But the other rebuked him, saying, "Do you not fear God, since you are under the same sentence of condemnation? And we indeed justly; for we are receiving the due reward of our deeds; but this man has done nothing wrong." And he said, "Jesus, remember me when you come into your kingly power." And he said to him, "Truly, I say to you, today you will be with me in Paradise." (Luke 23:39–43)

That good thief "stole" heaven. Imagine all the people he hurt, those he angered and who held resentment toward him because of the goods he had stolen. Yet he took responsibility for his misdeeds, felt sorry for having committed them, and realized that he deserved the punishment he was experiencing. He also witnessed to Christ's innocence and, by asking Jesus to remember him, joined his sufferings to Christ's and applied his redemptive suffering to those he hurt.

Purgatory allows the repentant sinner to share in redemption and so "complete what is lacking in Christ's afflictions" (Colossians 1:24). This doesn't mean that Christ's afflictions are inadequate—indeed they are sufficient to save the whole world—but it lets us know that we all need to pick up our cross and follow him: "If any man would come after me, let him deny himself and take up his cross daily and follow me" (Luke 9:23). Some of us do this in this life, while others run away from their cross. Christ doesn't give up on them; instead he offers them a chance to take it up in purgatory, thus healing the damage their lives have caused others.

When people we have hurt see how much we have suffered on their behalf out of love for them, I believe they will find it easy to forgive us the harm we have caused them. They will then look forward to the great heavenly banquet that the Father puts on for his prodigal children.

Catholics are not the only ones who believe in purgatory. For example, the famous Protestant theologian and philosopher C. S. Lewis wrote:

Our souls *demand* Purgatory, don't they? Would it not break the heart if God said to us, "It's true, my son, that your breath smells and your rags drip with mud and slime, but we are charitable here and no one will upbraid you with these things, nor draw away from you. Enter into the joy"? Should we not reply, "With submission, Sir, and if there is no objection, I'd *rather* be cleansed first." "It may hurt, you know."—"Even so, Sir."[10]

Lewis even emphasizes the voluntary nature of purgatory; souls *want* to go there to prepare for heaven.

QUESTIONS AND ANSWERS

I forgive, but I don't forget. Is that sufficient for God to forgive me?

God promises to forgive you as you forgive others. He also forgets what he forgives, as he says in Jeremiah 31:34. Let's imitate God's way of forgiving, since this is the kind of forgiveness we would like to receive.

Jesus says simply, "He who believes will be saved." If you believe in him, that's it! Heaven is guaranteed, right?

St. John explains: "He who believes in the Son has eternal life; he who does not obey the Son shall not see life, but the wrath of God rests upon him" (John 3:36). Faith, hope, and love are essential for going to heaven, but faith and love imply obedience, a union of our will with Christ's. So St. John says: "He who says 'I know him' but disobeys his commandments is a liar, and the truth is not in him; but whoever keeps his word, in him truly love for God is perfected" (1 John 2:4–5). Faith without works of obedience is dead (see James 2:14–26).

God wants us to avoid being too categorical about who goes to heaven and who does not. He, not we, shall be the judge.

Is purgatory something to be feared? How long does it last? Can a soul in purgatory still go to heaven?

Souls in purgatory are happy because they know they have "made it"; they know they are going to heaven. They want to be purified, because they know that once they are free of everything unholy, once all their sour relationships have been healed, then they will be with God and enjoy the happiness of heaven.

But this doesn't mean that purgatory is pleasant. It's a place for those who are not ready to see God when they die. Although the descriptions of this purifying fire are similar to descriptions of hell, there is a major difference: The souls going through this purification want to be with God and want to be with their loved ones.

Purgatory will last as long as it takes for a soul to be ready for heaven, ready to be in the presence of the all-holy God. In a way, it is for souls who are born into eternity prematurely—their relationship with Christ and with their fellow Christians needs to develop fully before such souls can "breathe" on their own. Purgatory is the incubator for preemies who need it to live outside the womb but are not ready to rest in their mothers' arms.

As I was growing up, my father described purgatory to me and my siblings, and then he told us, "Shoot for heaven, because if you miss, you have purgatory. However, if you shoot for purgatory and you miss . . ." Jesus gave similar advice: Seek first the kingdom of heaven and righteousness (holiness), and everything else will be given to you as well (see Matthew 6:33).

SIX

Purifying Fire

In the Sermon on the Mount, after describing the need to reconcile with those we have offended, Jesus describes additional ways we hurt others: with impurity and infidelity, breaking our word, seeking revenge, lacking generosity and mercy, hypocrisy, materialism, and critical judgments (see Matthew 5:27–7:6). All these things are incompatible with heaven.

Purgatory, then, is meant to burn away all the earthly attachments and attitudes that produce barriers between us and others and between us and God. Scripture often describes purgatory as a purifying fire that prepares us for loving and enjoying God and heaven fully.

NOTHING UNHOLY CAN ENTER HEAVEN

Heaven is a holy place, the blessing of an intimate union with God, where we will see him face-to-face. None of us are worthy of this honor. To be in the presence of the all-holy God requires us to be holy as he himself is holy (see 1 Peter 1:16) because "nothing unclean shall enter" heaven (Revelation 21:27). There is a great tension between being holy and blameless and the reality that we are sinners and need mercy. While only "the pure in heart . . . shall see God" (Matthew 5:8), we find ourselves constantly pulled toward impurity, selfishness, jealousy, and anger, even though we know that "those who do such things shall not inherit the kingdom of God" (Galatians 5:21).

That's why we need purification to make us "pure and blameless for the day of Christ" (Philippians 1:10). God wants us to embrace his purifying love: "Those whom I love, I reprove and chasten; so be zealous and repent" (Revelation 3:19). Although the purifying fire of God's love is unpleasant to us— even painful and repulsive—we can rejoice in it:

> Beloved, do not be surprised at the fiery ordeal which comes upon you to prove you, as though something strange were happening to you. But rejoice in so far as you share Christ's sufferings, that you may also rejoice and be glad when his glory is revealed. If you are reproached for the name of Christ, you are blessed, because the spirit of glory and of God rests upon you. . . . For the time has come for judgment to begin with the household of God; and if it begins with us, what will be the end of those who do not obey the gospel of God? And "If the righteous man is scarcely saved, where will the impious and sinner appear?" Therefore let those who suffer according to God's will do right and entrust their souls to a faithful Creator. (1 Peter 4:12–19)

Our purification is a sharing in Christ's suffering, so we can rejoice in the opportunity to become like Christ in all things, to take up our cross and follow him (see Luke 9:23) and endure "many tribulations . . . [to] enter the kingdom of God" (Acts 14:22). This is fundamental to the Church's teaching on heaven: "Those who die in God's grace and friendship and are perfectly purified live for ever with Christ. They are like God for ever, for they 'see him as he is,' face to face" (*CCC*, 1023).

PURIFICATION BY A CONSUMING FIRE

Many Christians experience a long, painful illness before death, while others seem to miss out on such potentially purifying suffering. But since "the glory of the Lord [is] like a devouring fire" (Exodus 24:17; see Psalm 50:3), we have the hope that as our soul leaves this earth, this devouring fire is capable of purifying it so it can enter heaven. Does God purify us in a quick, painful instant when we die? Or does such purification take place over a long period of time, perhaps because we cannot endure it all at once? Scripture simply doesn't reveal those details. What we do know is that anything unholy in us must be burned away before we can fully enjoy heaven:

> Now if any one builds on the foundation with gold, silver, precious stones, wood, hay, stubble—each man's work will become manifest; for the Day will disclose it, because it will be revealed with fire, and the fire will test what sort of work each one has done. If the work which any man has built on the foundation survives, he will receive a reward. If any man's work is burned up, he will suffer loss, though he himself will be saved, but only as through fire. (1 Corinthians 3:12–15)

When we die, God, who is a "consuming fire" (Hebrews 12:29), will purify us, burning away all our selfishness and pride. And then we will be ready to enter an intimate, face-to-face union with the all-holy God. This will take place in purgatory.

A passage from the Old Testament provides a good description:

> But the souls of the righteous are in the hand of God, and no torment will ever touch them. In the eyes of the foolish they seemed to have died . . . but they are at peace. For though in the sight of men they were punished, their hope is full of immortality. Having been disciplined a little, they will receive great good, because God tested them and found them worthy of himself; like gold in the furnace he tried them, and like a sacrificial burnt offering he accepted them. In the time of their visitation they will shine forth, and will run like sparks through the stubble. They will govern nations and rule over peoples, and the Lord will reign over them for ever. Those who trust in him will understand truth, and the faithful will abide with him in love, because grace and mercy are upon his elect, and he watches over his holy ones. (Wisdom 3:1–9)

The souls in purgatory are happy, because they know the purification they are undergoing will enable them to be with the God they love.

Think of it this way. Suppose you're relaxing in your backyard, basking in the sun. Then the doorbell rings and you answer the door, only to be surprised by all your friends, who are there to celebrate a surprise birthday party for you. But there you are, all sweaty, wearing your bathing suit, while they are all dressed up for the party! You're not ready—not in your bathing suit. You're somewhat embarrassed, but you need to get cleaned up, shower, and change into nicer clothes—even though you can't wait to join your friends and celebrate. This process of getting cleaned up is what will take place in purgatory when you're being purified.

God's purifying love helps us to put on our best clothes so we can enter the wedding feast. But to enter the wedding feast dressed as the bride, we need to be ready to give everything, to relinquish dominion over our very selves. In other words, we need to be ready to give our lives completely to Christ. Perhaps we are still holding on to some material attachment, or an unhealthy relationship, or old hurts and resentments, or whatever. Thus, the purifying fire of God's love helps us to let go of everything so as to give our whole selves—our very lives—to our Beloved.

It's Jesus himself who comes to our door and knocks! "[I]f any one hears my voice and opens the door, I will come in to him and eat with him, and he with me" (Revelation 3:20).

CONFIDENT HOPE TO SEE GOD . . . AND OUR LOVED ONES

Faith in God's love and mercy makes us confident in our eternal salvation. This goes hand in hand with Christ's call to be vigilant and watchful, so we won't be left out of heaven. We can be full of hope and confidence that Christ is preparing a place for us, and we remain vigilant so temporal earthly enticements and endeavors do not distract us from our heavenly goal.

We want to extend this confident hope to loved ones or acquaintances who have died, many of whom were not perfect or may have died carrying out a sinful act. Some of them may have left this world littered with a trail of pain, hurt feelings, and anger, disturbing the lives of family members, fellow workers, neighbors, and strangers with their words, actions, or inaction. Perhaps lingering resentment and animosity toward those they hurt makes heaven an unlikely prospect for our dead loved ones or acquaintances. Is there any hope that these enduring wounds could be healed? Could both the injured and the injuring reconcile and enjoy together eternal intimacy with God? Is there any hope that our prayer for them can save them?

Some believe that praying for the dead is useless—the dead are dead. If those who have died weren't saved already, then they have no hope. But Jesus, as usual, challenges our skepticism, telling us, "[W]hatever you ask in prayer, you will receive, if you have faith" (Matthew 21:22). Jesus says that our prayer is all-powerful when we pray in his name. He doesn't put limits on what he will grant us. He doesn't say, "I'll grant you whatever you ask, except . . ." No, he says "whatever" without any conditions or limits, and this includes the eternal salvation of our deceased loved ones . . . if we have faith. We can have confidence that Jesus will fulfill his promise: "Whatever you ask in my name, I will do it" (John 14:13).

The Bible also says that we should pray for all men, not just those who are alive: "I urge that supplications, prayers, intercessions, and thanksgivings be made for *all* men." Why? Because God "desires all men to be saved and to come to the knowledge of the truth" (1 Timothy 2:1, 4). God wants us to pray for *everyone*!

To summarize, while God calls us to be pure, holy, and perfect, we are not; we fall back into sin, which is totally incompatible with heaven. Yet Christ's promise gives our hope a firm foundation, and it gives us hope that our sinful but beloved deceased have a chance to join us with Christ in heaven and that with the help of our prayer the many wounds they have produced can be healed.

─────── QUESTIONS AND ANSWERS ───────

Does God ever replace purgatory with a long illness before a person dies?

This often seems to be the case. For example, God gave King Hezekiah a deadly illness as a kind of purifying experience, so he could receive God's mercy and be able to praise him forever in heaven (see Isaiah 38:1, 3, 9–20). Hezekiah himself spoke of his illness as a kind of purgatory: As he lay dying, he felt that he had been "plucked up" from the prime ("noontide") of his life and would no longer be able to "see the Lord in the land of the living." He asked for health, life, and forgiveness for his sins so he could be with God forever in heaven. God answered his prayer by healing his illness and lengthening his life.

Why should we pray for the dead? How could we change their fate?

Let's look at Jesus' response in the Gospel. His attitude toward the dead went contrary to those in his time who thought it impossible that the dead could rise:

> "You are wrong, because you know neither the scriptures nor the power of God. For in the resurrection they neither marry nor are

given in marriage, but are like angels in heaven. And as for the resurrection of the dead, have you not read what was said to you by God, 'I am the God of Abraham, and the God of Isaac, and the God of Jacob'? He is not God of the dead, but of the living." (Matthew 22:29–32)

In these verses, Christ teaches us to view the dead as living in God. That's why we should pray for *all* men and women, both living and dead. Jesus never condemned this practice but in fact prayed over the dead girl (Matthew 9:18–26), over the dead son of the widow of Nain (Luke 7:11–17), and over Lazarus, who was buried for three days (John 11:1–46). His prayers changed their fate. Perhaps our prayers can too.

Early second-century Christian writings mention praying for the dead. These early Christians considered it a natural consequence of their hope that the souls of the dead may join them and God in heaven, even though the departed souls have no possibility of repenting.

In addition, our prayers can help heal the hurt that sinners leave behind. For example, if the family of a murder victim still has anger and hate, our prayers for the murderer can help heal that family. This prayer manifests love, which "covers a multitude of sins" (1 Peter 4:8). Therefore "if any one among you wanders from the truth and some one brings him back, let him know that whoever brings back a sinner from the error of his way will save his soul from death and will cover a multitude of sins" (James 5:19–20). There always is hope for the sinner, especially one who loves and is generous with others.

FR. JOHN WAISS

But Christ prayed over the dead in order to bring them back to life. How can you compare that to us praying for the dead?

True, Christ prayed over the dead to raise them up to life. But we pray for the dead that Christ will raise them up on the last day: "The body is . . . meant . . . for the Lord, and the Lord for the body. And God raised the Lord and will also raise us up by his power" (1 Corinthians 6:13–14). Our prayer is that Christ will raise up our loved ones' bodies on the last day so they can enjoy eternal life with him in heaven. The miracles Christ worked by praying over the dead and bringing them back to life were a sign of what he plans to do with the resurrection of the dead.

No matter how hard we pray, those in hell cannot be saved. Isn't it better not to pray for the dead so we avoid contradicting Christ's promise to give us whatever we ask for?

God does not reveal to us who is damned and who is not. There's no way for us to know if any particular person has gone to hell. This means that when we pray for someone who has died, we are praying that all obstacles between him and God, and between him and others, are removed so that he can choose to be with God.

When we pray, we do not seek to change the mind and heart of God; we pray to become one heart and mind with him. Thus our prayer will be effective only if we embrace his will. As St. James tells us:

If any of you lacks wisdom, let him ask God, who gives to all men generously and without reproaching, and it will be given him. But let him ask in faith, with no doubting, for he who doubts is like a wave of the sea that is driven and tossed by the wind. . . . You do not have, because you do not ask. You ask and do not receive, because you ask wrongly, to spend it on your passions. (James 1:5–8, 4:2–3)

Therefore if we pray with faith for our deceased loved ones, seeking God's will, we can be confident in the effectiveness of that prayer and in Christ's promise.

SEVEN

Can Non-Christians Be Saved?

We hope and pray that our deceased loved ones will make it to heaven. Does this mean everyone will go? So many people have not been baptized or even had a chance to hear the gospel message, often through no fault of their own. Will they be condemned to everlasting punishment? And unbaptized babies who die, through abortion or miscarriage—wouldn't it be unfair for these babies to go to hell?

Before exploring these questions, let's remember that God doesn't want anyone to be lost: "The Lord . . . is forbearing toward you, *not wishing that any should perish, but that all should reach repentance.*" (2 Peter 3:9–10; emphasis added). We can confidently trust that God mercifully desires everyone to enjoy heaven, so let's pray for all souls, living and dead, and do our part in sharing our knowledge of the truth. There are souls waiting for the life-giving message you can share. As Jesus told us, "The harvest is plentiful, but the laborers are few; pray therefore the Lord of the harvest to send out laborers into his harvest" (Luke 10:2). Let's go into God's vineyard and complete the work assigned to us.

WHO WILL BE SAVED?

Curiosity about the afterlife is only natural: Who will go to heaven and who will not? What is the minimum I need to do to get to heaven? Will many make it or just a few?

Jesus doesn't want us to worry about these questions. He encourages us to focus on doing God's will instead. At the same time, he also warns us about the dangers of not making it to heaven:

> "Truly, I say to you, it will be hard for a rich man to enter the kingdom of heaven. Again I tell you, it is easier for a camel to go through the eye of a needle than for a rich man to enter the kingdom of God." When the disciples heard this they were greatly astonished, saying, "Who then can be saved?" But Jesus looked at them and said to them, "With men this is impossible, but with God all things are possible." (Matthew 19:23–26)

Notice that Jesus doesn't say who will or will not enter heaven. He only makes the point that it's hard for certain persons— such as the rich. Instead, he encourages his disciples to shed their materialism so as to enter by the "narrow door" or "the eye of a needle." He then reassures them that what seems to be impossible really isn't for God.

Jesus had a special warning for those who considered themselves holy—who ate and drank in his presence or listened to his preaching (see Luke 13:26–30), or those who prophesied, cast out demons, or did mighty social works (see Matthew 7:21–23). Christ warned that if these things were done without love, tax collectors and harlots would go to heaven before them. There is no free ticket to heaven—and there is no sin that God cannot forgive. What is required is love. Love is the essential thing.

JUDGE NOT!

We may have friends who are good people but not Christians. We might agonize over the prospect of where these good souls may end up in the afterlife. But Jesus told us, "Judge not, and you will not be judged; condemn not, and you will not be condemned" (Luke 6:36). We shouldn't judge or worry about what will happen with anyone, but simply make sure we are prepared:

> Do not speak evil against one another. . . . There is one lawgiver and judge, he who is able to save and to destroy. But who are you that you judge your neighbor? . . . [B]e patient. Establish your hearts, for the coming of the Lord is at hand. Do not grumble, brethren, against one another, that you may not be judged. (James 4:11–12; 5:8–9)

God is the judge, not you or I. It's not our job. When we begin to make judgments about who goes to heaven and who goes to hell, we are taking over God's role and duty. God does not take too kindly to us supplanting him! And if Jesus could forgive those who crucified him, then he can forgive anyone—even those who don't know him and his plan for salvation—just as he did the good thief crucified next to him on the cross. Jesus can grant this grace to any soul.

Only God knows what is in a person's heart; only he "searches the hearts" (Romans 8:27; Revelation 2:23). God "is greater than our hearts, and he knows everything" (1 John 3:20). We can trust that he will not punish anyone unfairly. Even souls who were ignorant of Christ will have an opportunity to see him in heaven: "They shall see who have never been told of him, and they shall understand who have never heard of him" (Romans 15:21; see Isaiah 52:15). We can confidently entrust all souls to God's mercy and let him do the judging.

OUR ATTITUDE TOWARD NON-CHRISTIANS

If it's possible for non-Christians to achieve eternal happiness in the afterlife, why should we bother sharing our faith with them? Does it make a difference what they believe, as long as they are living a reasonably "good" life? Instead shouldn't we be more tolerant of other people and their beliefs?

Think about it this way. Suppose you were in college and your best friend were describing this fantastic girl (or this fantastic guy, for you women) who he thought would be a perfect match for you. Your friend—who already has a girlfriend of his own whom he plans to marry—goes on to describe the person in great detail, including not just her physical traits, but her social graces, wonderful family background, professional and outside interests, etc. You then respond to your friend's description with enthusiastic excitement, asking him to introduce you to this person; perhaps you say to him, "I want to marry that person! Please introduce me to her."

But your friend says, "No, I think it's better for you to discover her for yourself. I don't feel right interfering in your life or in hers."

Would you consider that person to be your friend? No way. If he were your friend he would introduce you to the person who could possibly be the best match for you and offer you a lifetime of happiness.

Well, would we be acting like a good friend if we failed to introduce a person to his or her potential eternal spouse, Jesus Christ? Hardly! Christians have been given much, because God has chosen us and appointed us to be fishers of men and to bear much fruit (see John 15:16; Luke 5:10). And to "whom much is given, of him will much be required; and of him to whom men commit much they will demand the more" (Luke 12:48).

Christ tells us to teach others "to observe all that I have commanded you" (Matthew 28:20). He wants us to help others to embrace the fullness of his teaching. Let's not shortchange others, but instead let's freely share with them all that Christ has revealed to his Church.

QUESTIONS AND ANSWERS

If God wants us to live our lives so we can get to heaven, then why aren't we just born there?
What God wants is to build a family. He wants us to develop our gifts and talents and learn to use our free will here on earth. As our heavenly Father, he wants us to live for our brothers and sisters in this world, learning to serve them joyfully, working to support them in their needs, and creating such a family atmosphere that we will want to be with our brothers and sisters forever in heaven with him.

Some of God's children are physically or mentally disabled or challenged. But this gives the rest of the family the opportunity to love their sibling unconditionally, regardless of what that sibling can or cannot do. God calls us to face this challenge by overcoming our selfish tendency to think only about ourselves and our own wants, and to reach out to those in need, to give food to the hungry, drink to the thirsty, clothes to the naked, etc. "And the King will answer them, 'Truly, I say to you, as you did it to one of the least of these my brethren, you did it to me'" (Matthew 25:40).

Is God really as strict as it seems when it comes to getting into heaven?

What would you do if I said that he isn't, but then it turned out that he is? You would be upset with me because I let you down, especially if you didn't make it to heaven because of what I told you.

On the other hand, what would you do if I said that he is very strict, but in the end you found out that he isn't? You would reach heaven anyway and enjoy eternity there. You would have lived a worthwhile life, doing good for other people. You would have avoided hurting a lot of people because you chose not to be selfish, proud, or unkind. In the end, it would be a pretty good deal.

What will happen to good people who do not believe in God? Will people who have never heard about God or good people of other religions who really believe in their religion go to heaven?

God is the ultimate judge, not you or I. We must wait for him to reveal his final plan for each and every person. What he does want and expect from you and me is that we share our faith with those around us, giving as many people as possible the opportunity to hear the full and authentic gospel message. We want everyone to have the opportunity to love God and choose heaven for themselves:

> For, "every one who calls upon the name of the Lord will be saved." But how are men to call upon him in whom they have not believed? And how are they to believe in him of whom they have never heard? And how are they to hear without a preacher? And how can men preach unless they are sent? As it is written, "How beautiful are the feet of those who preach good news!" (Romans 10:13–15)

Do I have to believe in Jesus to go to heaven?

According to Christ's own words, "I am the way, and the truth, and the life; no one comes to the Father, but by me" (John 14:6). He is the only way; the Church has no other Bridegroom; only one bride enjoys the eternal marital bliss of heaven, which begins here on earth with faith in Jesus Christ. As the *Catechism* points out:

> Faith makes us taste in advance the light of the beatific vision, the goal of our journey here below. Then we shall see God "face to face," "as he is" [1 Corinthians 13:12; 1 John 3:2]. So faith is already the beginning of eternal life: "When we contemplate the blessings of faith even now, as if gazing at a reflection in a mirror, it is as if we already possessed the wonderful things which our faith assures us we shall one day enjoy." (*CCC*, 163, quoting St. Basil)

Again, Jesus says: "Not that any one has seen the Father except him who is from God; he has seen the Father. Truly, truly, I say to you, he who believes has eternal life" (John 6:46–47). The only way to see God in heaven is through Christ. As St. Peter pointed out to the leaders of the Jews: "And there is salvation in no one else, for there is no other name under heaven given among men by which we must be saved" (Acts 4:12). Jesus told us: "[A]s the Father knows me and I know the Father; and I lay down my life for the sheep. And I have other sheep, that are not of this fold; I must bring them also, and they will heed my voice. So there shall be one flock, one shepherd" (John 10:15–16). Let's let Jesus decide who these "other sheep" are and how they will be able to listen to his voice.

Did people who lived before Jesus' time have the chance to be saved? Are they in hell because they did not get to believe in the Good News?

When the Jews began rejecting Jesus because he was calling God his Father, he told them that even if they ignored him, he would preach to the dead and the dead would listen and have eternal life:

> Truly, truly, I say to you, the hour is coming, and now is, when the dead will hear the voice of the Son of God, and those who hear will live. . . . Do not marvel at this; for the hour is coming when all who are in the tombs will hear his voice and come forth, those who have done good, to the resurrection of life, and those who have done evil, to the resurrection of judgment. (John 5:25–29)

Thus those who died prior to Jesus' time got to hear his preaching and be saved, as St. Peter explained: "For this is why the gospel was preached even to the dead, that though judged in the flesh like men, they might live in the spirit like God" (1 Peter 4:6).

Did Jesus really go to hell?

The Apostles' Creed, the most ancient profession of faith, states: "He descended into hell, and on the third day he rose again." Here, hell—*sheol* in Hebrew; *hades* in Greek—is the generic abode of the dead where souls were deprived of the vision of God and were awaiting judgment. It's frequently used this way in the Bible (see, for example, Psalm 6:5, 30:3; Revelation 1:18), although sometimes these terms do indeed describe the fiery hell of eternal damnation (see Psalm 9:17; 16:10).

But Jesus has the capacity to release those who have died from their prison: "For Christ also died for sins once for all, the righteous for the unrighteous, that he might bring us to God, being put to death in the flesh but made alive in the spirit; in which he went and preached to the spirits in prison" (1 Peter 3:18–19).

Christ released the dead who truly loved him by giving them an opportunity to embrace his Gospel and to ascend with him to heaven:

Therefore it is said, "When he ascended on high he led a host of captives, and he gave gifts to men." (In saying, "He ascended," what does it mean but that he had also descended into the lower parts of the earth? He who descended is he who also ascended far above all the heavens, that he might fill all things.) (Ephesians 4:8–10)

Can an atheist go to heaven?

Again, the only one who can judge is God. I can imagine that some atheists, as well as agnostics (those who aren't sure about God and thus don't commit to believing in him or not believing in him), genuinely seek the truth but have been blinded from it for reasons outside their control, perhaps by hypocritical Christians. When they die and confront *the* Truth, they will have the opportunity to embrace him whom they have been seeking all their lives.

Let's leave each person's final judgment to God.

Where did Judas go when he died?

Although Jesus did say, "The Son of man goes as it is written of him, but woe to that man by whom the Son of man is betrayed! It would have been better for that man if he had not been born" (Matthew 26:24), this doesn't explicitly say that Judas went to hell. It would be better for us to admit that we do not know and let God be Judas' judge.

Where do animals go when they die? Will our pets be with us in heaven?

Jesus left many questions about death, heaven, and hell unanswered. Much of heaven will be a surprise for us.

But since God has made animals for us to enjoy in this present life, I can't imagine heaven without them. We won't "need" them as we do now, but they will be part of the joy and bliss we will experience in our complete union with God the Father.

Animals cannot enter into Jesus' marriage to the Church, which is the fullness of heaven. This means that our pets will not be able to experience heaven directly. However, because animals, especially pets, have been so much a part of our life and our earthly happiness, and God loves us so much, it seems likely that he would "resurrect" them and allow them to be part of our experience of bodily happiness in heaven. He wants us to be perfectly happy, and animals are part of being human and being happy as human beings.

If Noah's ark is a figure of our transit to heaven, then an ark filled with animals should be a consoling thought for those who love pets, since they were saved along with Noah and his family (see Genesis 6:1–8:22). Also, having our pets with us in heaven would seem to fulfill Isaiah's prophecy of God's judgment:

> And the Spirit of the LORD shall rest upon him, the spirit of wisdom and understanding, . . . He shall not judge by what his eyes see, or decide by what his ears hear; but with righteousness he shall judge the poor, and decide with equity for the meek of the earth; . . . The wolf shall dwell with the lamb, and the leopard shall lie down with the kid, and the calf and the lion and the fatling together, and a little child shall lead them. The cow and the bear shall feed; their young shall lie down together; and the lion shall eat straw like the ox. The sucking child shall play over the hole of the asp, and the weaned child shall put his hand on the adder's den. They shall not hurt or destroy in all my holy mountain; for the earth shall be full of the knowledge of the LORD as the waters cover the sea. (Isaiah 11:2–9)

EIGHT

It's Your Choice!

Heaven is real; hell is real. Both are an essential part of Jesus' teaching. Many people try to ignore the question of the afterlife, but eventually everyone has to face it.

We will truly begin to understand God, death, heaven, hell, sin, and salvation when we move beyond the dreadful legalism of just avoiding evil. While it's true that St. Paul lists what we must do to avoid judgment, just steering clear of these things is not what God wants for us. He has so much more in mind for each of us!

> Do you not know that the unrighteous will not inherit the kingdom of God? Do not be deceived; neither the immoral, nor idolaters, nor adulterers, nor homosexuals, nor thieves, nor the greedy, nor drunkards, nor revilers, nor robbers will inherit the kingdom of God. (1 Corinthians 6:9–10)

No, we must go beyond such thinking. We only truly understand heaven, hell, sin, and death by understanding how much God loves each one of us, how deeply he respects our freedom, and how earnestly he calls each one of us to enter into a personal, intimate, and unique relationship with him. We don't enter heaven by proving to God that we are somehow lovable, that we have performed our duties satisfactorily. We enter heaven by opening ourselves up to and accepting his love. By accepting God's love and being filled with his Spirit, we will naturally do good, avoid evil, and obey his commandments:

> As the Father has loved me, so have I loved you; abide in my love. If you keep my commandments, you will abide in my love, just as I have kept my Father's commandments and abide in his love . . . that my joy may be in you, and that your joy may be full. (John 15:9–11)

We shouldn't dread the afterlife, because it's meant to be a joy-filled, face-to-face encounter with Jesus. If we have befriended him in our life, then death will be an intimate encounter with our best friend. Even if we have ignored him in this life, we have nothing to fear because he is merciful and forgiving, even if unwisely neglected by us.

GOD IS PRO-CHOICE AND PRO-LOVE, SO CHOOSE LIFE

You have a choice. In the depths of the human person, man "himself decides his own destiny in the sight of God" (*Gaudium et Spes,* 14). It's a choice in response to God's love. God doesn't force us to love him in return. Love demands a choice, and God respects our freedom to choose him or to reject him:

If any one hears my sayings and does not keep them, I do not judge him; for I did not come to judge the world but to save the world. He who rejects me and does not receive my sayings has a judge; the word that I have spoken will be his judge on the last day. (John 12:47–48)

If we reject him, this is our choice, and God allows us to reap the consequences:

The nations have sunk in the pit which they made; in the net which they hid has their own foot been caught. The LORD has made himself known, he has executed judgment; the wicked are snared in the work of their own hands. . . . The wicked shall depart to Sheol, all the nations that forget God. (Psalm 9:15–17)

Hell is the pit the soul makes for itself with its own choices. Souls go to hell—Sheol—to escape from the God whom they have rejected and forgotten. God gives us this choice:

See, I have set before you this day life and good, death and evil. If you obey the commandments of the LORD your God . . . walking in his ways . . . then you shall live . . . and the LORD your God will bless you in the [promised] land. . . . But if your heart turns away, and you will not hear, but are drawn away to worship other gods and serve them, I declare to you this day, that you shall perish; . . . I call heaven and earth to witness against you this day, that I have set before you life and death, blessing and curse; therefore choose life, that you and your descendants may live, loving the LORD your God . . . for that means life to you and length of days, that you may dwell in the [promised] land. (Deuteronomy 30:15–20)

God asks us to choose to enter the promised land, which is a figure of heaven. He puts this choice before us now, while we are still alive, and he encourages us to choose the life he so deeply desires for us: "I set before you this day life and good, death and evil. . . . Choose life!" We choose life eternal by walking in his ways and serving him. Let's choose love. Let's choose life. Let's choose God.

NOTES

1. Joseph Ratzinger, Pope Benedict XVI, *Dogma and Preaching* (Chicago: Franciscan Herald Press, 1985), 62–3.

2. *Dichos* 64 in the *Catechism of the Catholic Church*, 1022.

3. John Paul II, *Mulieris Dignitatem*, 26; http://w2.vatican.va/content/john-paul-ii/en/apost_letters/1988/documents/hf_jp-ii_apl_19880815_mulieris-dignitatem.html.

4. Ratzinger, *Dogma and Preaching*, 116. See also Joseph Ratzinger, Pope Benedict XVI, *The Spirit of the Liturgy* (San Francisco: Ignatius Press, 2000), 59–61.

5. Jean-Paul Sartre, *The Words*, trans. B. Frechtman (New York: G. Braziller, 1964), 102.

6. In 1946 Pope Pius XII said that the sin of our time is the loss of the sense of sin. Pope Pius XII, "Radio Message of His Holiness Pius XII to Participants in the National Catechetical Congress of the United States in Boston" (October 26,1946): *Discorsi e Radiomessaggi di Sua Santità Pio XII*, VIII. Cf. also Joseph Ratzinger, *Seeking God's Face* (Chicago: Franciscan Herald Press, 1982), 16–19.

7. For Catholics, mortal sins are actions that completely break one's relationship with God, such as murder and fornication. Venial (non-mortal) sins hurt but do not break one's relationship with God, such as rushing through one's prayers or telling a white lie to avoid hurting someone's feelings; https://www.merriam-webster.com/dictionary/white%20lie.

8. Notes from a get-together with St. Josemaría Escrivá, July 6, 1974.

9. This does not mean that someone who has been abused should allow it to happen again. Along with forgiving the abuser, the heroic and just action often will be to report the abuser to someone in authority so that no one else will fall victim the abuser's wickedness.

10. C. S. Lewis, *Letters to Malcolm* (New York: Harcourt, Brace, Jovanovich, 1973), 108–9.

ABOUT THE AUTHOR

Father John R. Waiss received his bachelor's degree in mechanical engineering from the University of Notre Dame and a master's degree from Stanford, and worked three years as a design engineer and software developer. He went to Rome to study philosophy and theology, completing a doctoral thesis on Thomas Aquinas in September 2013. In 1987 he was ordained a priest for Opus Dei, a personal prelature of the Catholic Church dedicated to applying Christian principles to secular life and the workplace. His extensive work of guiding souls has included junior high and high school students (and their parents), college and young working men and women, and married people. He has been the pastor of St. Mary of the Angels Church in Chicago, Illinois, since May 2014.

THE
DYNAMIC CATHOLIC
INSTITUTE

[MISSION]

To re-energize the Catholic Church in America by
developing world-class resources that inspire people to
rediscover the genius of Catholicism.

[VISION]

To be the innovative leader in the New Evangelization
helping Catholics and their parishes become
the-best-version-of-themselves.

Join us in re-energizing the Catholic Church.
Become a Dynamic Catholic Ambassador today!

DynamicCatholic.com
Be Bold. Be Catholic.®